Praise for *The Good Culture*

"As talent leaders and practitioners, we spend years of our professional lives trying to create environments where our employees can thrive. We attend seminars and conferences, scour articles, trade best practices, try hot new concepts, and repeat the same old approaches, often all resulting in the same outcome. Rebecca Friese's book cuts through the noise and gimmicks to draw out what you really, truly need to know in order to build—and maintain—a Good Culture."

BETH KARLSSON, Head of Talent at Pinterest

"Rebecca Friese is a powerful voice for making things better. Her wisdom and insight have helped organizations large and small, and now she's sharing it with all of us."

SETH GODIN, author of *This Is Marketing*

"A connected culture is critical to loyalty, retention, and productivity. In this must-read guide, Rebecca Friese lays the blueprint for every leader to create their ideal culture."

MICHELLE TILLIS LEDERMAN, author of *The Connector's Advantage* and *The 11 Laws of Likability*

"Culture is the secret weapon of today's top companies. Think of *The Good Culture* as your owner's manual to that weapon. Creating a sustainable, successful business that attracts top talent and engages employees leads to delighted customers and an influential brand. Culture and brand are two sides of the same coin, and if you want to be a market leader, you'd better start from the inside out—with a genuine desire to connect to both employees and customers with empathy."

MARIA ROSS, founder of brand consultancy Red Slice and author of *The Empathy Edge*

"Culture is all about how you treat people: your customers, your employees, your suppliers, anyone who interfaces with you. Whether you are a large company or one just starting out, this book offers insights and practices that will be invaluable to building a Good Culture. Read it and make your company better."

MAYNARD WEBB, founder of Webb Investment Network and on the Board of Directors at Salesforce and Visa

"Culture is *not* a kombucha machine! Rebecca Friese does an excellent job articulating the simple to describe but hard to execute elements of a Good Culture. I could feel her insights, energy, and passion come through on every single page. A must-read for progressive leaders who believe their employees should thrive at work!"

ANNMARIE NEAL, partner and Chief Talent Officer of H&F and former Chief Talent Officer at Cisco Systems

"During this time of unprecedented economic uncertainty and the disruption of traditional workplaces, company culture matters more than ever. Rebecca Friese's blueprint to help leaders rethink their organization's purpose is a practical and well-written guide to help refine any company's mission and values, especially during this era of upheaval."

HEATHER CABOT, author of *Geek Girl Rising* and *The New Chardonnay*

"Organizations are transforming at rapid rates due to the continuous introduction of technology, requiring employees to reskill and upskill for jobs of the future. Recent research implies a link between workplace culture and an employee's ability to learn; learning in the new nature of work is critical to prepare for jobs of tomorrow. Rebecca Friese does a brilliant job highlighting the power of a Good Culture (with practical tools, tips, and applications) to ensure your organization is able to innovate, while minimizing disruption to your greatest assets—your people. If you believe in investing in your people, you must invest in providing a culture where you and your employees can thrive, and this book will give you the guidance to do so."

DR. JENNIFER NEUMAIER, Social Learning Researcher and Leader at LinkedIn Learning, a Microsoft Company

"If you are lucky enough to know Rebecca Friese, then you know her passion to inspire people to love what they do is her calling. It is thrilling to read the pages of her book and be transported back to the many lessons and learnings I've taken away from our almost decade-long partnership. *The Good Culture* is for anyone who wants their workplace to be anything but ordinary and offers the tools to help make it extraordinary."

DANIELLE SANDARS, Director of Global Communications and Employee Engagement at Converse (NIKE, Inc.)

"Rebecca Friese's book tackles the most essential question for leaders today: how can modern organizations drive their innovation and performance with their culture? With insightful stories from leading organizations like Whole Foods, Method, Zappos, and Workday, this book provides illustrative and practical stories as well as clear diagnostic and guidance tools. What does a Good Culture look like? What is your present culture? Where can you take your culture? How can you connect your culture in the everyday details (of management, recruitment, hiring, etc.) to the overall organizational purpose? *The Good Culture* can help with those questions and more so that work does not suck at your organization. I recommend this book to anyone leading an organization or aspiring to lead an organization today."

JAMES SHERRETT, Senior Technology Strategist at Slack

"*The Good Culture* is smart and critical. Rebecca Friese's message is clear: people are the priority. As a leader, creating the culture that enables your people to do their best work is your quickest and most likely path to success. Read this book."
KARA GOLDIN, founder and CEO of Hint, Inc. and author of *Undaunted: Overcoming Your Doubts and Doubters*

"Rebecca Friese artfully weaves together practical examples, storytelling, and culture facts to pull you in and take you on the journey to a successful culture."
STEPHANIE FITZPATRICK, SVP of Human Resources at UnitedHealth Group

"Love the practicality Rebecca Friese brings to culture change. It's simple to see that culture drives strong organizations, but driving lasting culture change is complex and difficult. If you've tried, you probably wished that you had someone or some resource to help you find the right path. Rebecca doesn't shy away from the reality of that complexity, but breaks it down with real examples, tools, and approaches to help you start asking the right questions to find a way forward."
KATE BROWN, VP of Culture and Engagement at a global financial services company

" 'There are companies that have Good Cultures, and there are companies where work sucks.' In Rebecca Friese's book, the case for creating a Good Culture is painfully obvious. But she shares a refreshingly obtainable path to getting there. In the years I've worked inside and outside of organizations, I've known this to be true— if your culture isn't good (aligned with your business strategy), it is unlikely you'll succeed. Rebecca's book makes this formerly 'fuzzy' goal of Good Culture clear for all of us."

JULIE HASSETT, Vice President, Chief of Staff, SaaS Engineering at a global enterprise software company

The
Good
Culture

The
Good
Culture

THE LEADER'S GUIDE TO
CREATING A WORKPLACE
THAT DOESN'T SUCK

Rebecca Friese

FLYN

ISBN 978-1-7348007-0-8 (paperback)
ISBN 978-1-7348007-1-5 (ebook)

Published by FLYN
www.flynconsulting.com

Produced by Page Two
www.pagetwo.com

Edited by Lisa Thomas Tench
Copyedited by Christine Savage
Proofread by Alison Strobel
Cover and interior design by Jennifer Lum

www.thegoodculturebook.com
#thegoodculture
#workshouldntsuck

For my family
Mom, Dad, Whit, Jen, Will, Staci,
Chris, Alexandra, and Thomas

I do this work so that everyone may experience what
it's like to be loved and supported as you've done for me,
even in the workplace.

Contents

Introduction

WORK REALLY SHOULDN'T suck, but let's face it—it often does.

We spend more than half our waking lives in the office, and driving there and back, five days a week. We spend more time with our coworkers than with our families and friends. We spend more time sitting at a desk than standing and moving around, which is jeopardizing our mental and physical health.

All of this is true for every one of us who works full time at an office job in the United States. And that's even before we actually get into the reality of working culture, your bosses' tendency to micromanage, or the possibility of downsizing due to a merger or to outsourcing overseas.

Work sucks big-time.

Why aren't we doing anything about it?

Worked sucked for me as well. Just out of university, I was working at my dream job for one of the biggest consulting firms in the world. In their change management division, they needed truly excellent communicators, and that was right in my wheelhouse. I credit that company with getting me to where I am today, because the knowledge that I gained about business and people and change was invaluable. But after five years of doing the same thing—enter client workplace, assess it, recommend the same old, same old strategy, rinse and repeat—I wasn't learning anymore and decided to move on. It was hard to justify walking in that same door every day when I didn't actually believe that my work was meaningful.

After yet another consulting gig, I was coming back to San Francisco from La Jolla on a puddle jumper and ended up sitting beside the twenty-nine-year-old founder of a start-up. Right then and there, after receiving an invite to a launch party that night, I mapped my career journey on the back of an airline napkin. By the end of that La Jolla project, which signaled the end of my consulting career, I was invited to become Head of People at the start-up, and I went from learning stagnancy to out-and-out freedom in a few months. The start-up was all ramp-up: I had moved from a company with sixty thousand consultants to a room with only fourteen people in an open-concept space, and I was tasked with bringing maturity and process into the room without killing their just-got-funded buzz. I was thrilled to be stretching my creative muscles, learning to work with autonomy, and scaling the company as part of their leadership team.

Soon after that, the founders hired a new, seasoned COO. But this change brought in a whole new set of challenges, as the C-suite's ideas of culture began to shift and rattle against each other. It was like working in a minefield, balancing clashing personalities, strategies, and cultural expectations. And then the dot-com bubble burst. Because we were paying too much attention to the culture clash, we were taken off course when we weren't ready. I had to start firing people. What I had loved about the company soon became what I disliked.

It sucked.

I was looking at all of these companies, successful and not, big and small. Whether it was my own company or a client, I would see things very clearly: people were just not jelling as a team. They phoned it in. They were exhausted and didn't feel like it was possible to achieve their goals. People were obviously and strangely angry at each other sometimes. There was backstabbing going on, but even worse, there was information hoarding: people would hide knowledge because they wanted to be the only one with it; people would decide not to tell others about their truly excellent strategic plans because they were afraid of being stopped in their tracks.

What was going on? Why were these truly excellent organizations, and their talented, wonderful people, hemmed in by this kind of behavior? Didn't they realize the damage they were doing to their own future success?

After realizing this, I did the smart thing decided to take a break. My new title? Queen of the Small Gig. My family had become a new priority, and I moved back to my hometown of Chicago, but I was still constantly booked as a coach, a solopreneur, a consultant. It wasn't until I got chosen for a three-day program called FeMBA (a mini-MBA for women entrepreneurs) with Seth Godin that things really started to click. Together with fifteen other women, I discovered the missing piece, the thing that connected the dots, the values that drove my interests and my excitement about work.

For me, my "why" came down to one single word.

Culture.

When it came to working with my clients, I realized that creating a great internal process is fine. Providing the team with tools is wonderful. But if you don't have a Good Culture in place, nothing happens. That was it. Culture was what I loved and what I wanted to do.

I moved back to San Francisco and got started.

After meeting Decio Mendes, who would eventually become my business partner in FLYN, I discovered that we could use design thinking tools and apply them to internal processes and management. We found out, through building forward and creating our own consultancy together where we really started to explore what mattered to people, that an organizational culture needs to align with strategy or you're going to be dead in the water.

The importance of culture is this: it is responsible for people's happiness at work, and people have to be aligned with it in order for it to work. If work sucked less for people, if we were more engaged and we truly wanted to come into the office every day, think of what we could do in the world! Our productivity quotient would be significantly higher, for one. We'd have less conflict on processes, and we'd more readily push ourselves out of our comfort zones. If we were all happy at work, what a different place this country would be.

But gaining a cultural advantage in an organization is not just about putting out a kombucha machine and patting ourselves on the back. There are a lot of mechanics behind Good Cultures.

That's what this book is all about.

Together, in this book, we're going to go through all of the steps that FLYN takes to dig into identifying organizational cultural values, creating alignment between values and strategies, and delivering on the promises that we make to stakeholders, especially employees. We're going to challenge ourselves to reveal what's actually happening at work so that we can move in the right direction. We're going to talk about the decisions we make, both explicitly and in hidden ways, that have an effect on whether or not our company cultures are helping or hindering the outcomes we want to see happen.

I'm glad you're on this Good Culture journey with me. If you're turning these pages, you're going to become empowered to make actual changes to your own organizational culture. It's actually something that is eminently possible: no matter how hard it may seem to turn a ship in an ocean of options, you can do this. But know that it's going to happen slowly. When people say you can easily transform a culture, I say good luck with that. Instead, we must understand, kickstart, nudge, and then carefully embed cultures. Whether you want an innovation culture, a supporting culture, a large or a small culture, it's open to you, and to your people.

And I'm here to support you every step of the way.

1

What Is Culture Anyway?

I T'S REALLY THIS simple: there are companies that have Good Cultures, and there are companies where work sucks.

It sounds like a very straightforward comparison, I know. But I really don't believe in a separation between good and bad. I'm not interested in simplification, but I am interested in exploring what makes some organizations thrive, stand out, and succeed in the most challenging of industries or communities.

And so, to me, there really is only Good Cultures and, well, everything else.

Your gut instinct probably tells you the same thing. We all know when the culture is not working—when it sucks. When I talk to people about the work that I do—building up companies' cultural resources so that people can do their best work—sadly, I get a resounding, "Oh, please, come help my company!" Every audience I've ever spoken to knows how to describe a Good Culture (supportive, engaging, energetic, innovative, productive, promotes learning) as well as a Not-Good Culture (demoralizing, demotivating, lack of trust, overworked employees).

I believe that a Good Culture powers strategy and success, through creating a work environment where individuals can thrive. In other words, I believe that work shouldn't suck. Unfortunately, it really does for a lot of people. They do not work in a Good Culture. The problem is that having a positive, productive corporate culture is something that many leaders strive for, but getting there, and staying there, isn't just about feel-good policies or Ping-Pong-table incentive tactics (you know what I'm talking about). The power of a Good Culture is something to behold, but the costs of a Not-Good Culture may be more significant than you might realize; missed opportunities, a lack of innovation, and poor performance in comparison to the market are all signifiers of cultural gaps.

So, what exactly is a Good Culture?

When it comes to business, culture can be defined in so many different ways, from the academic to the practical. By the 1960s we knew that there was such a thing as a corporate culture, but our definitions were grounded in ethnography: what people valued; what their social norms were; and even how they golfed, ate, and celebrated (after work) together. Now, understanding company culture is a lot more nuanced. Even talking about it can get people fired up: if there are norms in place, they might feel restricting or invasive, even unethical when it comes to managing diversity, for example, because that culture defines a way to do things that is based on who has the power (and not on who doesn't). Cultural norms may make change stagnant.

In fact, let's take a really straightforward example to unpack this invisible picnic basket of values and norms a little further.

How do you set a table? If you get together with a group of people to have a meal on a picnic table, how do you set it? Do you forgo cutlery or lay it all out for everyone? Do you use paper napkins, cloth napkins with napkin rings, or none at all? (Oh right, some people use napkins! A paper towel is a napkin, right?) Who gets to decide? In fact, who gets invited to the table at all?

All of these tiny little decisions are linked back to our social cultures and the power dynamics that surround them. And trust me, everyone decides differently.

So, let's make the definition of culture simple.

Taking all of the positive and negative aspects out of the conversation, we can easily say one thing: a culture is how things get done. Whether it's at the picnic table or at an organization, culture just is. It shows up in the way that the work happens.

We can expand this to talk about company cultures and what they're all about.

Let's look at a company that almost everyone has heard about before: IKEA. They've been able to demonstrate a high level of growth because of the fact that the company breaks all the rules. Lodging its finances under the protection of a nonprofit entity, focusing on the consumer experience so that customers feel like they are in control of the value of their purchases, and ensuring that customer fulfillment is immediate are some of the ways in which IKEA thinks differently than its competitors in the industry. From the point of view of customers, the company has set itself outside of traditional strategic models and allowed itself to reach further than other companies.

But the same can also be said looking at the inner workings of IKEA. From a technological perspective, IKEA's flat-pack shipping and distribution system is unlike any other in the industry. The company is able to save money by relying mostly on transportation by sea and limited land distribution. This also allows the company to limit the amount of money it puts toward delivery, as most consumers can pick up their own furniture within the stores' warehouses and take them home by packing the furniture in their own vehicles. The company has strict guidelines for how its designs are produced at its multiple manufacturing locations around the world.

But there are deeper reasons for its success. IKEA's stance on creating a learning organization through the advancement of social good is the cornerstone of who they are and what they stand for, in terms of their values. IKEA also leverages the ideas of thousands of worldwide employees and clientele, but the company bases its methods of responding to those ideas on organizational learning concepts.

What does this mean for IKEA's culture? They get things done through learning. They learned how to design, manufacture, and ship their products to a global community earlier than any other furniture company out there because they prize learning. That learning extends to their customers, who not only learn about sustainability through the flat-pack process and everything that IKEA explains in-store, but who also actually learn how to assemble furniture in their own homes as the result of IKEA's way of doing things.

Learning is IKEA's end-to-end culture solution.

The thing is, though, people don't necessarily want to talk about organizational culture in the workplace and what it means to them. Or they talk about it and have no idea what to do about it. In fact, in my experience, people often matter-of-factly state, "We don't have a culture here." But that's just not true. No matter what, there's a culture. It can be distributed, shattered, and dysfunctional. It can be helpful and inclusive or hidden and fear-inducing. It can make people feel good or it can make them feel disconnected.

In Good Cultures, people agree on what matters, and they align with it.

I believe that a Good Culture is a place where it is possible for team members to articulate not only what is nice to have, but what actually works in real life, in real time, for them to do their best work. A Good Culture, on the whole, is therefore responsible for people's happiness at work and the success of the company—because it works.

What works in building a Good Culture is taking an intentional, cocreated, and perhaps slower approach to business growth, where everyone in the organization becomes part of the effort and the outcome of striving for success. A high-performance culture is one that is able to demonstrate a high level of internal and external respect and responsiveness, where people, rather than profits, are the initial focus. Allowing people to feel empowered, both as employees and as customers, allows the lines between life and work to blur naturally rather than artificially, which ensures that they can be maintained over the long term.

When we think about the power of a Good Culture, we know that it's truly the thing that will power your strategy as a company. Here are three examples of why this is true.

1. If your corporate strategy aims to be innovative, and your top goal is to create many new products and iterations of old products, but your culture does not allow people to take risks because of a lack of psychological safety, then that won't work. You're not going to meet your strategic goals without alignment between your culture and your objectives.

2. If you know that performance and productivity is an issue due to a large percentage of your current workforce being actively disengaged, culture is the reason why you can't get things done.

3. If your company is growing and you're finding that attraction and retention are an issue, you need to be clearer on defining the culture that powers your strategy. The clearer you are about your culture, the more likely that the right people will come in the door and stay.

These three common issues are direct symptoms of a Not-Good Culture. Not only that, but both your existing employees and your potential new hires are going to sniff out your cultural issues. If you are aligned at work, what a different set of results you could create as a group!

In fact, that sense of alignment between your culture and your business objectives is something we're going to talk a lot about in this book. Alignment is really important, and it's not just one thing: we can create alignment of purpose, mission, vision, and values—up, down, and sideways, in every company. Without definition, clarity, and alignment, a Good Culture cannot exist. We're going to keep coming back to this idea of alignment and how it can be harnessed in the workplace.

Let's Dig In

In this book we're going to dig into the five tools that your company needs to create an aligned, authentic, and achieving company culture: a Good Culture. We're going to forget about everything else and focus on the really important stuff: the foundation of building the culture you need right now.

The five tools we'll tackle are:

- **Purpose Building:** Clarifying your North Star purpose in order to create true alignment between what you say about your business and what you're really doing, all the way down to the individual level

- **Culture Coding:** Figuring out "how things get done" in practical terms, in the day-to-day, and learning how to call out what isn't working

- **Culture-Add Recruiting:** Understanding that each person who joins your organization can be a culture-add or a culture-cost, and learning how to attract and recruit in the right direction

- **Deep Onboarding:** Bringing people into the fold in a way that supports cultural growth

- **Culture-Proofing:** Finding the right keys to supporting and developing people, from bottom to top, so that your culture works for you over the long term

It's absolutely possible to thoughtfully and intentionally create the culture you want and need in order for your company to succeed. And, in fact, I wouldn't just say it's possible, I would say that it's imperative. Here's why. According to Deloitte's most recent Global Human Capital Trends report (2019), 82 percent of employees said they believe that culture is a competitive advantage. As well, 94 percent of executives and 88 percent of employees believe a distinct workplace culture is important to business success. More than 50 percent of executives say corporate culture influences productivity, creativity, profitability, organization value, and growth rates. Having a culture that attracts high-quality talent can lead to 33 percent higher revenue.

And those statistics are only the tip of the iceberg.

Whether you've never even thought about these ideas before but think you might need to pay attention before something goes awry, or you already have a decent culture but just want to make it better, or you need a significant overhaul because you know there's a problem, you're in the right place. Here's where we get real about culture-proofing your organization's future growth and development.

How are we going to actually apply these ideas in practice?

In every chapter, we're going to run through the three sets of practices that you can do, right now, to support Good Culture opportunities in your day-to-day operations. Whether you have a large and complex business or one that's just getting off the ground, the focal points for building a Good Culture are going to be the same.

 Kickstarting. We'll talk about the actions you can take right away, driven by the people on your team, that can be done relatively quickly, with significant impact. These are ideas that you can implement right now for immediate, clear, and measurable results.

 Nudging. Once you've got your kickstart underway, I'm going to suggest thoughtful additions to existing processes in your organization that will help "nudge" your team's behaviors toward agility and alignment. This is going to require a bit of explaining. What is a nudge? It's any aspect of choice that alters people's behavior in a predictable way. But, in order for a nudge to work, it can't forbid any options or significantly change incentives. It's an intervention that must be easy for an employee to avoid. Nudges are not mandates; they are opportunities.

Let's take a really simple example of how a parent might nudge a child to take up reading. Putting wonderful books at eye level is a nudge, because it allows the child to easily see and reach them, and therefore the opportunity to read is made easier. Banning screens does not work, because it provides a reverse incentive. Children may actually resent books, and become less likely to read them, if they know that their parents are taking away their screens in order to force the issue.

When it comes to nudging, there is no such thing as a neutral design, however. While the organizing of things can help influence decision-making, positively or negatively, because many people are happy to accept the default setting in their environment, the choice options available to them also have to resonate. Adults are not children; they have agency and intelligence. That's why great nudging isn't just about setting a culture standard and creating a new system. Nudging is about creating easy pathways within existing systems that lead people to the desired action or behavior.

Nudging has to start somewhere collaborative and creative and unique to each company and its team.

Embedding. Long-term initiatives are also needed in order to truly address gaps in the organization to get to where you want to be, and we'll talk about what those look like.

At every step through this book, these three practices are going to pop up where and when you need to pay attention to them. We'll unpack these practices together as examples naturally arise, and you will start to understand the deeper meaning of what it takes to build a Good Culture. Using case studies from my personal experience, I'll show you exactly what can happen when organizations do (and don't) culture-proof their future.

Let's start right now.

2

The Power (and Costs) of Culture

CULTURE MATTERS MORE than we think, to our organizational capacity for growth and to the bottom line. At every level of an organization, there are going to be opportunities and barriers to supporting a Good Culture. The power of a Good Culture is something to behold, but the reality for many organizations is that any barriers are often, if not always, invisible.

We've defined what culture is, but we haven't talked about what culture means, at least in practical terms.

What does culture mean for organizations? Well, it's always going to be very specific to that entity, but we know a few key universal truths. First, it's about people, meaning that it is deeply intertwined with human resource management. Second, it is ubiquitous, meaning that it is everywhere and affects everything. Third, because it involves people and everything they do, it has an effect on the ultimate financial success of an organization. There is a deep and often obvious cost to a department or even to an entire company when we trace culture challenges back as far as they can go.

While Good Cultures are powerful, other cultures are as well, and we need to be ready to identify the difference as quickly as possible.

Here are two stories that reveal what happens when companies walk the talk of their cultural values, and when they don't.

The Power of a Good Culture

I was working on-site at Chevron, one of my clients, and rushing to a meeting—I was late. Moving quickly down the hallway from my office and around a corner, I jerked suddenly. There was an arm out in front of me, and I had to come to a sudden stop. I gasped, but there was a kind face behind the gesture.

"It's not that important," the person said, looking at the shock on my face. "It's okay. Please slow down."

Chevron exemplifies a culture of safety.

It's exactly what you think it is. A culture of safety is one in which all of the people in an organization are able to place a high value on safety and therefore simply do not act in an unsafe way, every single day. Many companies try to achieve this goal, but few actually do, according to field research. That's because it's a massive undertaking. For an individual organization's safety programs to work effectively, and to minimize accidents, all stakeholders' needs must be addressed, and the processes used by the organization must be integrated on a holistic level. Indicators for a safety culture include tests and measurements at the personal, the environmental, and the social-behavioral levels. This requires an integration of not just processes but personal attitudes of cooperation within an organization, and these attitudes need to link up to prescribed safety culture values and indicators.[1]

Safety has to be Chevron's number one priority, not only because of the risk of personal injuries at a large oil refinery or rig, but because of the fact that the nature of the industry means that hundreds, if not thousands, of lives—and the environment—are going to be at stake if safety isn't addressed. We all know what happened in the Gulf of Mexico when the BP oil spill led to one of the greatest human-made disasters of all time. Chevron learned from that experience, even if they weren't involved at all in what happened.

On a practical level, what Chevron knows is that there are three sets of processes that need to be in place so that a safety culture can be created. First, the people who work at the organization need to be vetted for their ability to fit into the norms of a safety culture through skills development, personality tests, and the support of their ability to adapt to new jobs. Second, environmental indicators need to be measured on a regular basis with ongoing checks and balances. Third, social-behavioral structures within the organization that can affect processes that have an impact on safety also need to be measured.

Chevron knows that companies which do not place a high focus on cooperation and caring about human lives are those that are likely to have more accidents. And so they care deeply about whether or not someone is in a rush, because, well, nothing is worth more than human lives.

So, even in the halls of Chevron's HQ, hundreds of miles away from their nearest physical plant, it's safety first.

Every single person in the company goes through drivers' training, even if the only driving they do is going to work. In fact, when you arrive on their campus, you'll noticed all of the cars parked backward in their stalls, because it's the safest way to orient in a lot. And getting from their cars to their offices, even when there is no traffic in sight, everyone uses the crosswalks. There are mirrors in the corners of hallways so that there is no chance of running into someone while you're getting to your next meeting.

In fact, Chevron starts every meeting with a safety moment. Whether it's sharing a personal story, or a reminder of where the fire exits are, or a news item about a safety practice gone wrong, the agenda doesn't get addressed until a safety narrative is shared. The company encourages their team members to complete peer-to-peer evaluations in each other's offices. If a cabinet is too close to a desk and you could run into it accidentally, you'll know about it.

At this company it's all about accountability. It's not expecting a lockstep approach to work; rather, it's recognizing what really matters and following through. If Chevron's team members don't follow safety culture expectations at their offices, they can't expect people on the rigs to do the same thing. It's part of a holistic effort to support everyone, every time.

And it shows something of value to their employees that sets the tone for their work: even in one of the biggest companies in the world, there are things that matter more than the bottom line—people.

CULTURE FACTS

It's not just employees who want a Good Culture. In fact, 78 percent of executives note that building a Good Culture would be one of the top five things that they'd aim to do if they wanted to add value to their organization. Only 15 percent of executives actually think their company's culture is on track, and 87 percent of organizations believe that culture is a significant challenge in terms of cohesiveness.

2015 survey of two thousand CEOs and CFOs, conducted by Columbia Business School and Duke University's Fuqua School of Business

The Costs of a Not-Good Culture

And now for the flip side. Here's what a lack of alignment looks like in real terms, and where a great job turns into a job that truly sucks.

A consulting firm with about 150 employees operated under a global, boutique brand. They catered to a top-tier clientele who paid a lot for their customized brand and product design and employee development services. Their values were linked to the firm's ability to roll their sleeves up and create highly customized solutions through collaborative innovation with their clients' employees and customers. In other words, their brand values were strongly tied to ensuring that everyone got along, and that good ideas were supported from the bottom up.

Behind the scenes, however, this company didn't deliver the goods. Or a Good Culture.

One employee there (let's call him Justin) was known as a top performer. A creative genius, in fact. Someone who was right there when the company was founded, taking a role in that flat organization, leading the development of his unit, never complaining. As well, he was a nice guy. Everyone loved working with Justin.

But then a new CEO came in the door, and he had a very different cultural style in mind. He came from a hierarchical business where command-and-control was the name of the game. The legacy employees had agency, but under the new CEO's rules, that wasn't happening anymore. People were micromanaged to the point where the CEO would personally check over senior staff members' emails and give them permission to send them out. Culturally, the company retained its value statements: they told the world that their values were all about people and supporting their growth, and that creative people came first. But that wasn't actually happening.

In fact, Justin felt the new CEO was so threatened by his openness and creative approach to business that he was setting him up to fail, left and right. Justin could deliver client work every time, but he was getting zero support in his development as a manager of people. Not only that, but other team members at the firm saw it happening. One day Justin was the head of a massive project, and the next day he wasn't. One day he'd be leading a team, and then the next day he wouldn't. His job description seemed to change every few months. On top of this stress, Justin was traveling almost weekly to work with some of the firm's biggest clients. No one seemed to be listening when he said he needed to broaden his team by adding some mid-level experts and spend more of his time mentoring younger consultants. It was always a matter of costs. It was very embarrassing for Justin, and for those who worked closely with him.

He weathered this storm for a few months. And just to underline his frustration, Justin started flying first class on the company dime rather than his typical economy plus, and his C-suite didn't notice.

Until months later.

That was when the company's accounting department told Justin's CEO that one of his intercontinental flights cost over $12,000. Justin was a good employee, and he didn't come into the firm feeling entitled or arrogant; in fact, his humility and care were reasons why he was so successful in his role at bridging communication gaps for his clients. So why did this high-flying employee feel so disconnected to his own company that he stopped caring? It wasn't that Justin didn't warn his CEO many, many times before about how he was feeling. It wasn't that the company lacked the knowledge to rout out the kinds of deep issues that get in the way of performance; they made their bread and butter doing just that for their clients. Was Justin's physical and mental exhaustion so intense that there was no way he could land that next deal without the comfort that flying first class could provide? Or did he start racking up his first-class points because he wanted to get his bosses' attention in the only way that they would understand?

The job sucked for Justin, and it sucked for his firm.

Some people might assume that when a case like this comes to light, it's because there's not enough control being leveraged on something like expense management processes. Or that the employee needs to be brought into line. But what if, instead, we're seeing an employee simply reflecting the company's culture? The company's stated values said that they were all about collaboration, but what they seemed to want more than that was control and financial austerity. The company's CEO, indirectly, gave Justin leeway to buy a lot of expensive plane tickets, when what he really wanted and needed, for his clients and for himself, was the actual support to do his job well—in the form of resources, development, and autonomy.

Bottom line?

A company culture determines how people get things done, as we've already established. This company's decision makers tacitly communicated to the whole team that how people got things done was on their own, with no support. In fact, it was the opposite of support—the message was that everyone needed to be out for themselves if they were going to be successful. In Justin's case, he didn't have budget approval over new hires, but he did have an ability to determine his travel budget without oversight. This firm's culture wasn't in alignment. Then they expected Justin to comply with unstated cultural and leadership values rather than the brand values they told their clients about. It's not surprising that Justin felt a little lost.

Was Justin right or wrong in making this decision? Did he deserve those expensive airline tickets, or was he completely out of line?

Here's the thing. It actually doesn't matter.

Justin's CEO could have avoided this course of action in the first place if he had given Justin the development support he needed on projects and as a leader instead of setting him up for failure. He could have turned his challenge into a win by supporting him, which would have led to even greater productivity from Justin, and possibly new clients. He could have even rewarded Justin's innovation and incentive and tested his ideas with other consultants who worked on high-priority projects. But he didn't, and the cognitive dissonance between the values Justin was selling to his clients and the values he was expected to follow inside company walls was visible to those who were paying attention.

CULTURE FACTS

A full 47 percent of people who are looking for a new job are doing so primarily because they are disappointed with their company's culture. They are so unhappy with the culture that out of these leavers, 71 percent would be willing to take a pay cut in order to get into a company with a better culture fit. This is contrary to the fact that 89 percent of bosses actually believe employees quit because they want more money, which is clearly not the case. Employees' ideal culture? One that is marked by open communication, strong leadership, and work-life balance. In fact, 58 percent of people have left a job, or would consider leaving, if the company's culture was weakened by negative office politics. That's because intangible benefits and day-to-day experiences at work have risen in importance to US employees. People don't just come to work for a paycheck; they want to feel good about what they are doing.

Hays US "What People Want Report," 2017; Randstad survey, 2018

It All Starts at the Top

A big part of the reason why Chevron has been success-ful in achieving an amazing level of culture alignment is because their leaders are aligned with the idea of culture work, and a big part of why Justin made self-serving deci-sions was because his corporate leadership team didn't value that same alignment.

What are the repercussions when not just one, but many employees feel the same way and are making deci-sions that aren't aligned with the values of the company and therefore are not serving its goals?

We can't imagine that there's only one Justin in a misaligned company. There are many more misaligned companies than we often realize, and we can't always guess when these kinds of alignment challenges are going to crop up. In the United States, for example, according to Gallup's 2017 State of the American Workplace report, 51 percent of employees report not being engaged—meaning, in their terms, that they neither like nor dislike their job. LinkedIn and Imperative's most recent Work-force Purpose Index, which was published in 2018, found that 58 percent of companies with an articulated, under-stood sense of purpose experienced over 10 percent growth, compared to 42 percent of companies that don't make purpose a priority. And 25 percent of employees state that they don't know much about their company's mission or values at all.

Let's unpack this a little bit. Leaders have personal traits. They also have beliefs, feelings, and habits. They have their own view of the world, and that view shapes their decisions.

So far, leaders are like any other human beings on the face of the planet.

The thing is, however, that leaders make decisions which affect other people on a daily basis, not just themselves. Their ideas about what matters and what doesn't have a deep effect on the culture of their company, as well as on the day-to-day actions, feelings, and habits of their teams. But when leaders' ideas become negative idiosyncrasies, namely beliefs that (through any other lens outside of their own) seem unhelpful or ineffective or, at the worst, painful for others, then there's a cultural issue at stake.

Leaders' opinions matter on a scale of significance much higher than those of any other individuals within their organization. Organizational leadership is so important to the life of a company because it creates a sense of purpose and a vision for the future within that community, in which people can learn how to apply best practices. It is not enough to provide a set of instructions for employees on a day-to-day basis. This, in and of itself, does not constitute leadership. Instead, the point of organizational leadership is to create the impetus for individuals to find their own pathways to achieving goals, both for themselves and for the organization, so that they can feel connected to their work.

Let's get real about why this is something we ought to be transparent about. The impact of leader idiosyncrasies on culture (and success or failure) is so prevalent in business that academics actually have a name for it: upper echelons theory. This theory tells us that leaders are more likely to make decisions that fit their own unique interpretations of the world than they are to make decisions solely in the best interests of a company. If a leader's worldview is aligned with the culture and strategy in which they are working, they will be successful, and if it isn't aligned, they won't be. Most of the time, however, this is an invisible issue.

Good Cultures are those where leaders listen, and I mean really listen. We all have a tendency to listen with the intent of replying rather than with the intent of understanding. We're generally either speaking or preparing to speak, most often considering what the other person is saying only based on our own experiences and points of view.

Listening can also be broken down into five levels:

1. **Ignoring:** not listening at all.

2. **Pretending:** "Yes. Hmm. Right." (What we say when we are really thinking about what happened on *Game of Thrones* last night.)

3. **Selective listening:** Hearing only certain parts of the conversation (usually just the parts we want to hear).

4. **Attentive listening:** Paying attention and focusing energy on the words that are being said. (And then immediately going to the old standby: "I know exactly how you feel; when that happened to me...")

5. **Empathic listening:** Getting inside another person's frame of reference, with the intent of true understanding. Seeing the world the way other people see it allows us to understand how they feel.

Good Culture leaders listen to what their team members and their customers say about how they experience the organization: what it's like to work there, and what it's like to buy there. They use empathic listening. Of course, it takes a great deal of security to go into a deep listening experience because we open ourselves up to be influenced. We become vulnerable. Defensive communication is of the lowest level and comes out of low-trust situations when we don't want to be vulnerable at all. It's characterized by combativeness, protectiveness, and legalistic language that prepares for the eventuality that things may go wrong, that people may become resentful. Respectful communication, on the other hand, is characterized by honesty, authenticity, and respect.

And this can happen at any level. Strategic leaders in Good Culture companies aren't always those who remain in the upper echelons of an organization; rather, they are the ones who are able to learn, adapt, and adjust, moving in and out of specific roles and communities of practice within their company, and building relationships with these listening and communication skills. Not only do leaders need to be aligned with the culture, they also need to be supporting and displaying those behaviors themselves, as well as rewarding, recognizing, and communicating the behaviors that align with the desired culture.

And let's face it. You can't just start over. You're not going to fire your whole C-suite or management team to get the right culture fit, nor can you force employees to feel good when there's a natural conflict between what's being said and what's being done. This is not to imply in any way that all people in leadership positions are (or aren't) so myopic that they can't see the forest for the trees. But what we'll find, in reading the examples in this book, is that sometimes folks at the top need to commit themselves to leadership and followership in order to find those nuggets of cultural opportunity that are right there in front of them.

Getting on the Bus

When it comes to culture alignment, you're either on the bus or you're not. If you really believe in your company's values, are you actually making them work? Or do you see evidence of work sucking for people who matter to your organizational success?

When we take culture seriously, we have to set aside the expectation that a company's brand and marketing values are all that matter. What actually matters to a Good Culture is that the external values that you purport to have, and those that you practice at every level, day to day, are actually the same values as the ones needed to support the organization. And by this I don't mean that the company ought to create an unreasonable, external, marketing-oriented set of values and then force every employee to take an oath that they will "live the brand." That's also not going to work. It's a transactional point of view, and it's a short-term approach that simply doesn't land with anyone—employees or the market.

A long-term approach (and one that, perhaps unexpectedly, is more likely to result in financial success) is focused on building leadership alignment with the organization's culture, at the same time as team alignment with the organization's culture is being introduced. Misalignment in business happens all the time, and the possibility of business myopia that ignores the concerns of customers or employees means that a new culture process can hardly be achieved by relying on old organization norms, so change has to take place.

We can work toward revealing the cultural symptoms that are signs of a need for a shift, but sometimes this becomes a standard organizational change process that doesn't look at the whole picture of why certain values matter inside company walls. That's why creativity methods like design thinking don't have to remain in the toolboxes of engineers and software developers. In fact, we can use design thinking—something we'll explore quite a bit as we move forward in this book—to help our organizations determine the gaps between what's stated about the company and what's actually happening culturally.

We can also start on the path to creating our own culture by intentionally exploring and explicitly defining
what our purpose is as an organization.

3

Purpose Building

Designing Your Culture

So many companies start with what they are selling rather than why they are building a business. To make the right impact, there is a need for you to start with understanding your "why," as Simon Sinek has eloquently noted. Your "why" is not just about product differentiation, but also the differentiating factors your organization communicates outward so that customers, clients, and employees understand why your organization exists.

Ask yourself these questions:

- Does your company have its long-term goals, values, vision, and mission written down?

- Do you have a clear understanding and awareness of your company's talent assets as well as its challenging behaviors?

- What focus area is at the heart of your company's business strategy right now?

- Do you believe that the company already has the power to move toward its long-term goals?

- Do your company's responsibilities seem like barriers to achieving your collective goals? What's standing in the way?

Now, think for a second about what your company and brand values are. What do you tell people your company is all about? What do the vision, mission, and values statements posted on your company's website say about what you do and what matters to your team? Then think about what is actually valued, rewarded, and recognized in the company. Your company might say you value "customer first" practices, for example, but does your top-tier salesperson, who sells products to customers that they don't need, continue to get a bonus at the end of every quarter versus the salesperson who is honest with customers about what they need or don't need and therefore doesn't make the same number of sales? It's not that it's the salesperson's fault. These kinds of values are ingrained, often impossible to see or define, and therefore really challenging to address.

You'll be able to see a pattern emerge quickly if you drill right down to what's actually happening and what you want to happen. What's the difference between the two lists? And what's the weakest link—time, money, process, physical effort, mental effort, or routine—that's preventing alignment between the two?

Kickstart Your Purpose

Explore your current state by asking employees, leaders, and customers what they believe the purpose of the organization is. Survey them. Brainstorm it out. Pay for their lunch and then really listen. Why do your stakeholders think the organization exists in the first place? Write their responses down. In fact, write up your organization's origin story, seeking out employee feedback and cocreating it with them. What was the need you were meeting in your community or industry, and why did the founders think it was something that needed to be addressed?

Wells Fargo is an example of what can go wrong when there's a lack of alignment between a company's culture and its unstated values. The implications of this misalignment have put them deep into the forest for many years.

In 2016 the Securities and Exchange Commission (SEC) fined Wells Fargo $185 million for fraudulent activity. Research into the company's activities found that, after their acquisition of Wachovia during the global economic crisis, Wells Fargo pressured employees to cross-sell a number of different products, to the point where employees described the bank as a "grind house," with coworkers "cracking under pressure." Firings were frequent when employees couldn't make the grade, and as a result of the pressure of the sales goals, employees started creating false customer accounts as a means to make their quotas. Even whistleblowers were fired, surreptitiously and illegally, as they tried to keep the company aboveboard. Between 2011 and 2016, the actual number of firings topped fifty-three hundred. After the SEC investigation, CEO John Stumpf resigned, unsurprisingly, but it took that happening for the sales quota system to be abolished. The good news? Wells Fargo is taking sweeping actions to course-correct and realign across the board—from changes in leadership, processes, programs, rewards and incentives, and even their workplaces.

Preparing people to thrive in a Good Culture begins with knowing your starting point. Building connections between self-awareness, employee needs, business needs, and customer needs means that you have to know exactly where you stand, right now. Creating and maintaining a Good Culture starts with looking under the hood at the mechanics of it all.

Real-Life Good Culture: Caliber Collision

Caliber Collision CEO Steve Grimshaw recognizes and understands that accidents take people off their path in life, and his company's job is to get them back on that path as quickly as possible.

Think about it. When people are involved in an automobile accident, they may be at a critical juncture in their lives. They may have to deal with a significant injury, a temporary or permanent loss of work, or even the death of a loved one. Even if someone doesn't have to deal with this kind of tragedy, they're likely going to have to deal with a financial outlay or time wasted dealing with insurers and finding short-term transportation accommodation.

CULTURE FACTS

What's the financial cost of a Not-Good Culture? According to a massive research effort by The Conference Board, Mercer Sirota, the ROI Institute, The Culture Works, and Deloitte Consulting LLP, cultural issues at work cost US companies up to $550 billion a year. And employees know it. In fact, 95 percent of employees understand the moment when a culture isn't working. Even though most of these employees are clear about culture fit and its impact, they aren't always willing to bring it up with their companies because of the challenge of getting management buy-in for change.

The Conference Board et al., "DNA of Engagement: How Organizations Can Foster Employee Ownership of Engagement," 2017

Someone who comes into Caliber is someone whose day is not going well.

At a typical autobody company, let's face it, trust and compassion aren't always high on the list of priorities. Most autobody shops are transactional, flipping as many cars, and customers, as they can. They want to get people in and out fast because that's how they amp up their bottom line.

Because Caliber Collision understands this sentiment, their purpose is a practical one: "to restore our customers to the rhythm of their lives." As they say, they're not just fixing cars, they're fixing lives.

Okay, on the surface, their mission seems a little unexpected (if not outright weird) for a company that's growing so fast that investors are queuing up to line the kitty. It's a bit more Lion King than Wall Street for an internationally oriented organization. But I need to say it again: Caliber's mission is a practical one. Why? Because the rhythm of life is why the company exists. If people weren't on the road, moving quickly, trying to reach their own goals but once in a while truly failing at it, then Caliber wouldn't have work to do. They benefit from others' mishaps, and therefore the company believes that it has a responsibility to be understanding, ethical, and principled about their work.

"How would you take care of a client if they were someone you love? If it was your mom? Or if you don't like your mom, your sister or daughter... someone else you love?" Grimshaw posits to his employees when making the rounds to the shop floor, the front desk, and the accounting offices of his company. He and his team hire people who support each other, and who act on these heart-centered principles at home as well as at work. It's a prerequisite for the team to be principle driven rather than process driven.

The deep alignment and resounding financial success that Caliber has found as a result of their commitment to their principles doesn't have to be as revolutionary as it sounds. You can nudge your company culture toward alignment. Acknowledging the fine art of nudging is your second step forward, but you may not be clear on what it actually means in real terms.

Nudge Your Purpose

Start by communicating your purpose, and a reminder of why you are doing what you are doing. Whether at an all-hands meeting or in emails, explain all of your decisions going forward by connecting them to back to this organization-level "why." Reiterate the purpose on every communication platform: your website, your documents, your recruiting page, and anything that customers, employees, or potential new hires may see.

In looking closely at Caliber Collision, their work is inspirational because it doesn't start with a financial vision. It starts with actually helping people, including those in need of their services and those who work within its walls. The company is also helping the communities in which it operates, and not just in ways that match its industry or marketing goals: Caliber puts food on tables for people in need through its support of food bank programs. It's all about building out from that one purpose.

This approach is changing the vision of the autobody industry, where, let's face it, people feel screwed and trapped on the regular. It's shifting the expectations of employees and customers alike for what they can expect from a company, because the purpose is embedded through every level of the organization. Getting back into the rhythm of life is something, however, that everyone can understand with clarity, and so it's easy to apply to each decision and each fork in the road as the company expands toward a global presence.

🌱 Embed Your Purpose

Use your purpose as a lens through which to look more deeply at programs and processes throughout your organization: do they help the organization achieve your purpose or hinder your progress? From there, make a road map of those things that need to change to create further alignment, building this number one criterion into all decisions. Think about how broadly you might be able to expand your purpose over the course of many generations of doing business.

4

Culture Coding

Open Sesame

N 2O17 GOOGLE engineer James Damore wrote an internal memo after attending a mandatory diversity program. On the surface, he agreed with some of the findings cited in the program, namely that women were not receiving the same career support at the company as men, and that this was problematic. Nonetheless, Damore subjected the program to intense scrutiny because, as he said, its ideas represented an "ideological echo chamber" that, in his opinion, created reverse discrimination against men. In his point of view, the differences between men and women were biologically based rather than socially ingrained. Therefore, Damore stated that he needed Google employees to understand that women's inherent neuroticism, among other things, stood in the way of their success, and that Google should aim to make them more "comfortable" in the workplace.

He was fired within a month.

Damore filed a complaint with the National Labor Relations Board (NLRB), but this firing was deemed legal

and justifiable due to the letter's "harmful, discrimina-
tory, and disruptive" statements. At the time, Google's
CEO Sundar Pichai reminded employees: "To suggest a
group of our colleagues have traits that make them less
biologically suited to that work is offensive and not okay."

Damore's criticisms of Google's handling of the program, on the other hand, were valid, according to the
NLRB. Employees should be allowed to inquire as to
the efficacy of internal training. In fact, according to
a follow-up on the case published by *Wired* magazine,
Google's internal forums showed some support for
Damore; *Wired* reported that there were employees who
were afraid to come forward about this issue, and that
they expressed their thanks to Damore in private as well.[2]

When it comes to culture, whether these employees,
including Damore, are dangerously clouded by their own
bias or not is beside the point. It should be expected as a
given that company leaders will have to engage with this
kind of debate in an increasingly polarized US political
climate. There is a cost to not directly addressing these
challenges (especially in a very large company such as
Google), which is that employees feel as if they have to
create their own niche cultures within an organization in
order to feel safe.

This is the reality, therefore, in that there are surface
cultures in organizations as well as an underlying culture
or cultures. In one respect, Damore is certainly correct:
Google expected people to be in lockstep with its chosen
surface ideology.

CULTURE FACTS

Culture is key: 38 percent of workers want to leave their jobs due to a toxic work culture or one where they don't feel they fit in, and more than half of workers don't believe that their culture allows them to thrive. But 71 percent of employees admit they stay in their current jobs because it's easier than starting somewhere new. That means that many companies are filled with employees who simply don't want to be there and don't feel as if they have incentives to perform, other than just staying the course.

Harvard Business Review, 2019

If there is a strong culture at an organization, what happens to those who don't fit in, for a range of reasons? The cost of exclusionary cultures is that they can create, unintentionally and sometimes for the best of reasons, a negative underbelly that doesn't allow for a range of voices and opinions. That kind of culture may be just as psychologically unsafe as one that discriminates openly, not because it engages in reverse discrimination, but because it doesn't allow for the kind of open dialogue that solves problems proactively, before manifestos are written and posted to thousands of coworkers.

We can't get to a place of culture cohesion when people feel like they can't share who they are, what they think, and how they are internally reacting to the chosen values of the company. In the case of Damore, what he personally didn't grasp was that the essential issue at stake wasn't about inclusion or diversity; it was about alignment. And what Google didn't understand was that there was an alignment gap already present before Damore took the diversity program. Why did the situation escalate so quickly and become such a cultural touchstone for people inside and outside of Google?

What Damore was ultimately saying through his memo was that he was feeling unheard and unable to voice his opinion. For him, work really sucked, and Google, in not addressing this ahead of time, was affected deeply.

What's a Culture Code?

A culture code is the explicit, written-down set of agreements that your organization lives by. The values. The "we will" statements. It's not just what's defined in your purpose and mission, though. Writing a culture code is a way of illustrating what these primary documents mean for a company and how they ought to manifest every day. It's not an unchanging thing! A culture code can grow and scale and change. We can eliminate what we don't use, nudge intentionally, and move in any direction.

Creating Psychological Safety
Is Your Number One Goal

In any culture, building trust through transparency and communication is necessary if you want to nurture your cocreators and nudge effectively. If you are trying to nudge a culture, there can be no overcommunicating of your culture code messages. Those will be the pillars that people lean into. Because, as my cofounder, Decio Mendes, has said, in the absence of information people will connect the dots in the most paranoid way possible. And by extension, if someone chooses not to work for the company because they aren't aligned with those messages, that's actually okay. Clarity leads to alignment of values and, by extension, a focused purpose.

And let's be real. Google might be a poor example of how alignment works. There's a status that is associated with Google that probably resonates outward more than its actual culture, one that is based on its size and impact in the field of everything web. This may be the reason that Damore didn't quite fit in the way that he thought he would: he wanted to join the biggest and the best, and he didn't think about what working for Google would actually mean, culture-wise. But that places an even bigger onus on Google. Why did Damore get in the door in the first place? How was he chosen for his job? Was culture fit a part of the process or was the company just looking at his engineering credentials alone? How was Google communicating its culture, its expectations, and its values?

CULTURE FACTS

Respect lays the foundation for an inclusive culture, and the opposite leads to burnout. A 2018 Gallup study of nearly seventy-five hundred full-time employees found that 23 percent of employees reported feeling burned out at work very often or always, while an additional 44 percent reported feeling burned out sometimes. In addition, American workers forfeited nearly 50 percent of their paid vacation in 2017. That means about two-thirds of full-time workers experience burnout on the job, leading to employees who are 63 percent more likely to take a sick day, 23 percent more likely to visit the emergency room, and 2.6 times as likely to leave their employer. Gallup linked these findings back to company cultures that lacked the right mindset, tools, processes, and managers. They say that when employees do not trust their manager, teammates, or executive leadership, it breaks the psychological bond that makes work meaningful.

Gallup Workplace Poll, 2018

This isn't to say that the Damores of the world, full of fervor for their own point of view, should have the ultimate say on how a culture ought to work, but the door has to be open for conversation or for employees to either find their individual way in an organization or to exit gracefully if, ultimately, the culture is one in which they cannot do their best work. Ideally this will happen without the 24-7 global news cycle becoming involved.

Companies can hire highly motivated individuals, but another thing to acknowledge is the way that they fit into the culture of a workplace is also linked to the determining factors behind psychological safety.

Managers need to be there for their employees, being supportive and providing encouragement and help, but without taking the employees' work on themselves or micromanaging them. This suggests that self-analysis (understanding our own motivations rather than those of others) is more important to organizational success than simple active listening. Whether the goal of the organization is to develop its workforce to decrease turnover, support innovation, or develop a strategy for succession, the connection between motivational interests and success needs to be taken into consideration at the same time as other human resource planning practices.

For example, business research shows that there are differences in level of engagement according to various demographic indicators that can have an effect on the level of psychological safety that a person will experience in the workplace.[3] People who are younger than twenty or older than forty have a much higher likelihood of feeling engaged in their workplace, most likely because of a lack of experience and a greater enthusiasm, when it comes to young people, and a sense of confidence and self, when it comes to older people. Critically, this means that when people are in the middle of their careers, when businesses need their energy and experience the most, they may be the most difficult to engage in building and maintaining a culture code. As well, people who have a range of life responsibilities, such as younger parents who are also in the middle of their careers, may also have difficulty feeling fully engaged at work because of a lack of support at home.

These are real barriers to psychological safety that business leaders need to pay attention to. A culture code can't work with only those people whose work-life balance skews to a significant degree toward work, or those who never experience isolating or alienating experiences at work. If these challenges are overwhelming your employees and work is sucking that badly, then you have bigger issues at stake.

Companies need to be aware of all of these factors so that they are able to create the right support systems for their employees at these critical times in their lives. Values need to be created around and with the whole of the company, not just those who have an interest in putting their hand up. It's not realistic to simply hire people in certain age groups or without any psychosocial issues at all. There are always going to be these challenges at stake, even in the best of companies and people. Even so, employees have to feel a level of psychological safety in order to thrive, and companies have to be realistic about the ways in which external challenges will always affect their team members and the energy they have to contribute to the values of the organization.

As one employee said about his horrible former employer's culture, "I just needed leadership and HR to give me what I needed to do my job and then get out of the way. Instead, they did the opposite. I was made to wear 'party hats' and attend 'team-building' events, versus just getting me the approvals and support I needed to get the job done. As a top performer I was literally punished for not participating in the 'culture' in the way they felt was 'right.'"

How can we sum up psychological safety? First, employees need a combination of autonomy and direction, consisting of both measurements and goals that can be attained in a cohesive team environment. Second, knowledge resources including job skills, training, and information, but also human resource tools such as compensation and office materials and supplies, need to be consistent and focused on what employees actually require in order to do their jobs without feeling precarious. Finally, teams need active forms of support, including approval, self-esteem balancing activities, and constant feedback and encouragement from the leadership and management team.

Kickstart Your Culture Code

Ask your employees for stories of where they see your organization's values show up, or where they might be in conflict (stories of opposite behaviors). Let them be real about what they believe. This helps people get to the meaning of the "values in action," versus just words. And keep asking. Sometimes the first words out are those that leaders want to hear, rather than what folks really think. It's worth inviting people into the culture conversation many times in order to discover what really matters to them.

Real-Life Good Culture: Kronos

Kronos, a workforce-management software company, has been around for forty years, but it still considers itself a start-up.

That's because CEO Aron Ain, author of *WorkInspired*, places a huge emphasis on Kronos's people: even though the company is big, it's always morphing into something new, something innovative, and the company's teams are invigorated every day they come to work. The thing is, even though the company seemed to have a Good Culture, it wasn't defined anywhere specifically, and people described it differently, both internally and externally. Kronos was growing and changing so much that they believed it would be valuable to codify just what it was that made their culture great, so that they could continue to nudge in that direction, rather than somewhere else, somewhere unknown.

When we got involved, we engaged with Dave Almeda (Kronos's Chief People Officer) and his team, who were already experiencing immense success in increasing engagement through their programs and initiatives. We sought to understand what makes Kronos great, at its core, so that Almeda's team could build off that with an eye to the future—nudging their organization intentionally toward even more success on the basis of their current and past success. After interviewing hundreds of people and discovering how they experience their culture, what they believe in, and what is actually true about the company versus what the company says about itself, we found out one key thing. The company didn't just have a set of values that everyone communicated to each other; they had principles. Employees had a clear, shared idea of what they knew to be true about life and about work, rather than just a set of leading ideas of what they thought ought to be important.

Once those principles were on paper, the plan was that they needed to be embedded everywhere. The Kronos website. The recruiting platform. Internal programs and processes. Performance management. Kronos's goal was to communicate and reiterate what their culture meant to them so they could move toward a level of alignment that few organizations achieve. This isn't about getting employees to drink the Kool-Aid, either; it is about getting the right cultural information from employees so that Kronos could invite new people in the door, either clients or new hires or collaborators, who wanted to do work with a company like theirs. As well, they could close any culture experience gaps that were discovered in pockets around the organization. The Millennial in Indiana who feels disconnected from the social aspects of the work culture at HQ needs to feel just as linked to the culture as those in the C-suite.

Nudge Your Culture Code

Align a few aspects of your rewards and recognition programs and tools with the values and begin deploying them right away. This could be a simple shout-out at a team meeting, a fun physical object that gets passed around for the embodiment of a value, or an actual award. Always accompany these recognitions with the story of the value in action so people get to see examples of desired behaviors that get rewarded.

Open Up

As we've been talking about, employees aren't likely to share what they really feel about their workplace unless they have a semblance of safety in doing so. No one is going to say that they think that their company has a flawed culture out loud unless they have a safety net in place. Developing an open and honest feedback-driven culture is something that every company ought to support so that issues can be unpacked and addressed as they arise, not when it becomes a crisis for an individual or for an organization.

CULTURE FACTS

What's in the way? According to one survey, 52 percent of human resource leaders say that management lacks buy-in to actually make the changes that are necessary to build a cohesive culture. This includes, more than anything, ensuring that employees have a work-life balance. That simply doesn't happen, when 72 percent of employees are bringing work home on a nightly basis or over the weekend. And although 43 percent of workers are stressed to the point where it is affecting their health, half of companies seem to be unwilling to do anything to help change things for the better.

HR.com survey, 2017

Because psychological safety is so important to cultural success, leaders' "soft skills," like openness and emotional intelligence, truly impact the bottom line.

But this goes two ways.

First, companies have to create the impetus for people to feel comfortable in sharing their feelings, especially as they relate to everyday operations, and the leaders' ability to understand and work with human emotion is critical. Emotional expressions provide information to help individuals within a conflict situation to know and comprehend others' ideas, beliefs, and intentions, and leaders have to embrace knowing and honoring these reactions. It's all about finding those pain points so that companies can become aware of disconnects between people and the organization's purpose, find a solution, and converge. Emotions, in this way, are a good indicator rather than a barrier: they signal a need for change.

Second, and maybe this is even more important, companies have to provide support for a personal development culture so that people can work with and through their own emotions in a way that is productive. In other words, self-awareness and other-awareness are a big part of the culture equation. Employees have to be aware of their own triggers and barriers to communication in order for Good Cultures to really take hold, and for alignment to settle. In fact, research shows that when people learn self-regulation and openness on the job, and when individuals have the ability to make decisions for themselves, performance goes up.[4] As individuals learn how to find their own path and are motivated to take agency in their own work, they begin to seek out solutions for more and more complex problems, including person-organization fit.

🌱 Embed Your Culture Code

To truly embed your culture code, you have to dig down even further into the principles or guideposts behind your values. These are the ideals you know to be important and true to your company, and the commitments to actions and behaviors that allow employees to understand the meaning behind each value. It's important to define each value to this next level so that you can create the specific actions, behaviors, and decision processes you need to actually guide people in the right direction. If left too vague, with too much room for interpretation, they are ineffective. For example, if you say that "transparency" is one of your values, what are you committing to with your employees, your customers, and your shareholders? What are you not committing to? Once you've agreed on these guideposts, use them to assess current programs, processes, and future decisions. Are you doing what you committed to? If not, make a plan to change!

5

Culture-Add Recruiting

Culture Creation Is Cocreation

C ULTURE STARTS WITH who gets to come in the door.

We all tend to think about culture as something like a behemoth: it's bigger than us, it's stronger than us, it just is—we have no ability to impact it as an individual. But the reality is that culture is about people, and therefore the fit between people and organizations is really critical. Culture isn't big and scary; it's individual and intimate.

All that having been said, creating the right person-organization fit might be a little more complex than one assumes. Field research on recruiting shows that it is necessary to ensure that each person is compatible with a role and has the best match between the organization's needs and their knowledge, skills, and abilities (KSAs) linked to specific job requirements, but recruiting also has to be linked to overall social development within each organization.[5] This is especially true for a knowledge economy like the United States, because ignoring the needs and values of individual employees and other organizational factors has an impact on organizational development. As a company grows larger, the cumulative impact of person-organization fit becomes an even more critical aspect of human resources—and of the ability of the organization to adapt to new ways of managing change.

We want to generate high-commitment employment practices so that employees are drawn in, stay in, and feel like work doesn't suck. In other words, culture has to begin with leaders deeply examining what this culture contract ought to be, and how it is communicated to potential employees, before the organization begins to recruit for its new needs. This is because these social and psychological concerns are likely to dominate new employees' ideal workplace.

How does this work? Recruitment best practices begin at understanding how to best reach out to a diverse labor pool, with the goal of finding that culture alignment. Questions you'll need to ask yourself are:

- Where do these pools exist? Where can they be recruited?

- What is necessary for understanding the sociocultural language spoken by the people whom you want in your culture?

- How can target groups best interact with the internal human resource team through open communication?

- How can we avoid "more of the same" while attracting those who align with our culture?

We're not just talking about online recruiting by using values-based keywords on LinkedIn. You probably already know why that won't work. The role of human resources is changing because of the advent of techno-logical means of recruitment, employee assessment, and task management. With moves toward big data, mass customization, and gamification in the workplace, HR professionals will need to look at different ways of doing business and keeping ahead of the curve, but we're relying on systems more than ever before to gauge the viability of candidates for jobs, when, really, everyone has a differ-ent language. It would be great if your company's value system used the perfect words to find ideal candidates, but that doesn't allow for the natural nuances of human communication. Finding the right folks for your orga-nization is going to require you to dig a bit deeper into the process of recruiting. What's going to work, not only logistically but realistically, for finding the people who will actually matter to your growth? Therefore, there is a need for leaders to address bias globally while still being able to maintain a humanistic, needs-oriented approach to these tasks within a new focus on culture alignment.

Planning requires, as well, the need to look at moti-vational factors and extrinsic benefits that appeal to your target recruits so that these can be included in com-munications. How can your management team place an emphasis on aligning organizational and employee needs without setting aside a review of core skills? That having been said, think about reaching people for culture alignment rather than a regimented idea of what an employee in your company looks like based on their résumé alone. Is there any flexibility that the company is able to offer—for example, job sharing, time flexibility for people who have family demands, external development opportunities for those who may not yet have earned a degree, or cross-training initiatives that will build skills for new employees' résumés, and any other opportunities that will allow for diverse needs that can be communicated in human resource postings?

It's also important to think about the ways in which individual applicants at the company are supported through the interview process, and whether they accept the job. All barriers to person-organization alignment ought to be addressed along the way. This also means that the recruitment team ought to vet the program and its success over the course of multiple recruitment cycles.

 ## Kickstart Your Culture-Add

Engage people in the recruiting process who are already great examples of your culture. Think about the everyday champions who exemplify the behaviors and actions you desire in future employees, and get them involved in recruitment planning and interviewing, even if it's not their primary role. They will naturally attract those with similar values.

CULTURE FACTS

What works to build culture? Peer connections. In fact, 89 percent of HR leaders agree that ongoing peer feedback and check-ins are key for successful outcomes when it comes to building culture. Creating supportive feedback environments is critical to culture. That's because ensuring that employees' voices are heard needs to be part of a larger push for creating a Good Culture. In addition, culture and empathy are inextricably linked, as employees are unlikely to feel truly respected and empowered in an organization that does not show empathy. Inviting more people to the table, and creating ways for people to share their stories and ideas, is a win-win for everyone.

SHRM/Globoforce Employee Recognition Survey, 2018

Real-Life Good Culture: Juniper Square

Juniper Square, founded in 2014, suddenly received $25 million in Series B funding to fuel the growth of its commercial real estate investment platform.

The challenge was, they had to ramp up fast. With only forty employees in place, they knew that this funding, like it had for so many other start-ups before them, could break the organization as much as it could provide them with the floating capital they needed to level up.

Everyone loved working there and loved the culture, and they needed to create a culture code before they started recruiting.

Cocreation was their goal, and Juniper Square took up the call to action like no one else. We interviewed; they reviewed. We opened up the review to employees, literally every single one of them, so that they could give feedback and see where the problems might lie. We did that again. And one more time. And then one more final time with the leadership team.

Everyone had their say, enough so that founder and CEO Alex Robinson stopped and said, "Hey guys, I can take it from here."

At some point in every process, leaders have to own the culture. This company cocreated with a passion, and then Robinson took their culture code from 85 to 100 percent and put it on paper. That's when he went back to the team to get their input on how to activate it in real terms.

This process, for Juniper Square, doesn't end there. It's an iterative process to deliver on their culture code, every step of the way, as the company lives up to its expectations.

 ## Nudge Your Culture-Add

How do people know who you are and what it's really going to be like working with your team? This is where your culture code really matters. You need to be crystal clear about what you are, not what you want to be, if you want to land new hires with person-organization fit. Add a section on your website and/or in your recruiting materials that describes your culture, including examples of what people do inside the inner sanctum and out there with your customers and clients. Right away, this will help attract the talent you desire and the people who will want to work in a place like yours over the long term, so that you can minimize turnover and all of its costs.

Your Employees Are Your Cultural Guides

Your employees are your guides to building a culture.

Here's where it gets fun. Cocreation is necessary not only because of the act of recruitment itself, but because it's so important to look beyond recruitment to building a motivational and performance-enhancing strategy for human resource management that begins before the individual has been hired and continues throughout the employee's tenure there. A company can't simply look at the fit that personality will provide; they also have to look at how they can continue to engage with each individual throughout their career span so that they can achieve their goals as an organization.

Let's take, for example, the Workforce Management Initiative (WMI) at IBM. It's essentially about how the company uses and places its people's talents. The aim of the WMI was to engage in a new way of thinking about business and talent development through a value creation process, in which human capital could be integrated on a global basis, and where knowledge could be leveraged and shared depending on the needs of the organization, its customers, and other stakeholders such as shareholders. The WMI is therefore a means by which labor and skills can be placed within a set of value chain parameters that allow the organization to optimize its use of the workforce, and to create and shift models of work to accommodate for each shift in the company's strategy over the long term.

It sounds like IBM is putting people into a computer and spitting out data, rather than real information about people.

But are they?

The WMI shows that it is possible to scientifically assess and deploy talent as needed, and that it could be beneficial to the organization to manage the supply and demand of talent within each department and within the company as a whole. Nonetheless, the company recognized that in order to do this, it would be necessary to create a new language, and a new set of cultural norms, around the process. The taxonomy of talent supply and demand, suffused with this data, would then provide the framework for the optimization of the human resource network within the organization.

But IBM needed people to like it and use it in order for the WMI to work.

Companies aren't always going to feel the same way about how to approach psychological safety. Culture also has a lot to do with how people perceive stress, and therefore there isn't one strict way to build toward comfort in the workplace. If managed well, this approach would allow employees the chance to expand their influence in the organization as well as their skill sets in working with different teams on a project basis, which could be a benefit to their motivation. It could therefore allow employees new scope for expanding their roles in the organization, and for taking on new challenges, which could lead to higher job satisfaction and retention over time. Think about it: using this system, employees could be seconded into a short-term internal consulting role in another country, or connect with an ideal job before it was placed in the recruiting queue, or register for a professional-development program that they had never heard about, because the system kept track of all of those ideal placements, wants, and needs. IBM's system made employees happier, more productive, and more successful in reaching their personal and corporate goals.

For a company like IBM, this approach is aligned with their culture code, and that's why it works. The company is big, it's about hard-core computing, and it creates taxonomies all over the place. That's why it works. IBM understands what works for their people. And that's why they went in this direction.

And where's the bottom line in this equation? In the present-day global market, a strategic business orientation that effectively perceives the nature of complexity in what we do (serving different cultures and social groups, adapting to the personalization and rapid communication of the Internet, innovating at a rapid-fire pace), emotional intelligence is a tool for adaptability and knowledge creation. A global point of view in business is one that understands other people. Understanding other people results in engagement, revenue, and profits.

To do this, we each also have to understand ourselves and why we think the way that we do. But for this to work, leaders have to create the ultimate psychological safe zone, so that we are okay with exploring our ideas in comparison to other employees, to the company leadership, and to clients and consumers.

CULTURE FACTS

What matters when it comes to different age groups? While 77 percent of Baby Boomers are going to stay right where they are, more than half of Gen X and Millennial employees are on their way out the door because cultural norms are set by older team members who have power and aren't letting the culture adapt to openness, honesty, and flexibility. But the cost of turnover is high, starting at $15,000 for entry-level employees and going up from there. It's easier, and likely much less expensive over the course of many years, to create the right foundation for culture in the first place.

Deloitte's Global Human Capital Trends report, 2018

If employees are reacting to your own internal initiatives with fear or derision or absences, then something isn't aligned. And in organizations where leaders think they know better than employees about what matters, engagement will fail. What are you role modeling for your team, in cultural terms? Being brave enough to work with employees on culture, and cocreate it with them instead of trying to control it, is important. Let employees have their fingerprints all over it and they will be naturally be engaged.

If you really understand the power of alignment, you'll know that getting to alignment means your employees are your cultural guides. In fact, field research shows how important this perspective on employees really is.

Letting your employees be your cultural guides is a bottom-up approach that builds your team's intelligent risk-taking, growth, change, trust, and ownership.[6] Successful human resource leaders need to ensure that their team members feel strong and capable enough to give it their all and exceed their own and the organization's expectations. Employees' KSAs (knowledge, skills, and abilities) need to be noticed and respected each day on the job. Leaders have to develop a genuine interest in how others do things so that they can learn from workers as well, and capitalize on what makes a culture work well.

Culture-adding has to be seen as an end-to-end strategy rather than something that stops once the employee contract has been signed. You can give people individual accountability, but it only works authentically if you give people the power and the voice to make their vote count.

It's also about teamwork. Sharing of social experiences is a necessary component of positive outcomes in the workplace, and if individuals believe they do not matter to an organization, they will directly disengage. Companies have to be able to flip the script to a values-based approach to engagement in which meaningful relationships are created between individuals at different levels of the company so that people have relative autonomy in their decision-making process and feel as if they have the right to be a cultural guide. Autonomy allows employees to ensure that they have both the tools they need to succeed and the impetus to use those tools in a way that benefits the company community. In placing importance on well-being rather than just achievement, however, a company can create a positive work climate. This can increase the level of creativity, internal and external helping behaviors, and job satisfaction in the company, which can, in turn, result in organizational success.

In order to create a Good Culture with a cohesive team atmosphere, however, autonomy has to be balanced by support. Employees need to be able to be oriented toward the kind of self-discipline that autonomy offers, but they may not be able to achieve this goal unless they are given the opportunity to feel supported by the management team or by their peers. Leaders have to strive to establish an environment in which teams are given the space they need to develop innovative opportunities that build upon their members' varying expertise and skills. If employees are able to be recognized for their skill sets, then it is likely that their self-esteem will be bolstered in the same way.

Real-Life Good Culture: Whole Foods

Whole Foods' interviews don't start and stop with human resources.

The company's values are all about transparency, something that Whole Foods still strives to maintain even after their Amazon merger. Everyone's salaries are on display, including the CEO's. There's a democracy in place that lends itself to everything the company does, from departmental decisions to training. Everything is regional, as well; the Whole Foods model means that every store is run as its own business, with the team leader of each store being responsible for his or her store's profits and losses. Individual regions manage stores in their area because of the value of knowing their local customers.

For this company, hiring new team members happens through panel recruitment, but not a table made up of higher-ups and human resource directors. Departmental team members are invited to participate and, in fact, lead these panels. Anyone from any department might be sitting at the table in addition to field experts (members from the cheese team, for example, might be required to jump on board if a specific knowledge set is required). And it's the same for internal and external hiring: employees may or may not have their own teammates on their panel.

And here's the best part. Whether or not a person gets hired requires complete consensus. One person's veto, no matter what role that person plays in the company, can result in a pass on a candidate. In addition, each new employee goes through a three-month probationary period, at the end of which any team member can voice their concerns about the new employee before they get voted on the team full time.

That's what a company means when they walk the talk. When Whole Foods says that everyone has a voice, they mean it. The team is in charge, and they take their hiring roles seriously.

🌱 Embed Your Culture-Add

There are two major parts of your attraction and hiring process that need to be culture-coded. The first part is how your organization shows up and is talked about externally, and also your recruiting approach, which includes individual employees "living" the culture but also the process by which you interview and make decisions on hires. Externally, you'll want to look at things like Glassdoor, LinkedIn, and your website to make sure that the story potential candidates are seeing matches what you want to project. The second part is what happens inside the organization. Internally, you're going to want to make sure your process, in and of itself, reflects your values (democratic? open? transparent? geeky? creative?). Then, you'll want to embed certain practices

to evaluate your culture-adding efficacy. Many organizations design interview questions around their
values; others train specific individuals to dig into culture
alignment during interviews so that culture-adding
becomes natural.

6

Deep Onboarding

No Compromises

AT NEXT JUMP, when company leader Charlie Kim was challenged on his stated commitment to treat everyone on his team like family, he doubled down. Kim instituted a no-fire policy. That's exactly what you think it means. No one at the company, no matter what they do, can actually get terminated for performance issues. The result: lifetime employment for every single person in all of the company's four global offices (illegal activities notwithstanding, of course). Once you're in, you're in.

Let's go back a few steps.

With their headquarters on Fifth Avenue in New York, Next Jump is, at least on the surface, an e-commerce company. Their role in the greater scheme of global business is to serve up exceptional loyalty programs for twenty-eight thousand merchant companies like Dell, AARP, Intel, and Hilton. With fewer than two hundred employees on the books, their team works hard to ensure that all of their systems work seamlessly and that their corporate partnerships are thriving. It's not an easy business to be in; not only does the tech have to be seam-less, but the programs they sell have to work for millions of consumers. This means that Kim and everyone on the Next Jump team has to understand people: what matters to them, how they think, and, perhaps most importantly, how they feel about the brands they favor.

Kim's point of view on business is grounded in the fact that his company has weathered some of the biggest storms affecting e-commerce start-ups when others have failed, folded, or sold up. By the late 1990s, Kim's dorm room idea had turned into a company of 150 employees, only to downshift to only four people a decade later after the dot-com bust. Building Next Jump back up again meant that he had to create a strong sense of trust, in both directions. People wary of working for start-ups needed to be convinced to come on board, and Kim had to make sure that he had the right people to rebuild. To him, that meant only one thing: leverage his commitment to his team and bet everything on them, their time, and their ability to imagine a new future.

That's why, a few years later when Kim brought in a new advisor, he stopped to listen when this person asked him a very important question, one that would shift the trajectory of the company forever: "if you say that you treat everyone like family, why would you fire people?" That's a good question, but one that most company lead-ers would assume had a single, obvious answer. You know what it is. It seems ludicrous to even consider building a company when you can't fire whomever you want, when-ever you want. There are limits.

CULTURE FACTS

Getting on board may be tricky. Only 12 percent of employees strongly agree that their organization does a good job of onboarding, and they blame their managers when that doesn't happen. Managers account for 70 percent of a company's cultural experience for workers, and according to the same research, they are the number one reason why individuals leave an organization for greener pastures. In fact, 58 percent of people say they trust strangers more than their own boss. Now that's an issue that needs to be addressed.

Gallup Workplace Poll, 2018

Here's the thing: Kim didn't see those limits. He didn't limit his thinking, because he felt that there was something more he could do to actually build forward, and therefore the idea of a no-fire policy wasn't a constraint. He chose to double down because he saw an opportunity to align Next Jump's values and actions, and his instinct told him that it was the right thing to do, not just for his employees but for the company as a whole.

A strange thing happened, however, once he presented the policy to the team. People stopped hiring for their departments. Teams became frozen in fear. This was something they had never experienced before. The natural response to a lack of firing was a lack of hiring: no one wanted to be responsible for hiring that one person who just didn't work out, if the company was stuck with them for life. What if flaws in the hire only became apparent three months into their tenure? What if new hires didn't understand how to navigate the company's very distinct culture? What if their skills weren't up to par for what Next Jump expected them to take on? What if they just weren't a good fit for the company's global partners?

Kim's response? To double down on his double-down.

In order to ensure that people were ready to take on their roles, Next Jump created a boot camp. Once a person is hired at Next Jump, they're required (and fully paid) to take on a several-week onboarding process that helps them build their self-awareness, address any development needs, and learn about Next Jump's business needs and customer service expectations right out of the gate. This level of understanding—not only how the business works but also how employees work as individuals and what they need to accomplish personally, rather than just professionally—allows new hires to fully immerse themselves in their new roles. Sometimes, and perhaps often, people go through the Next Jump boot camp more than once. This isn't seen as a negative. Each person has to feel ready, and the team has to feel confident in that person's readiness, to take the next steps forward. Only then will they start their new role.

That's not the only thing that Kim did to make his company one of the most successful in their field. In 2016 a team of Harvard professors published research in their book *An Everyone Culture* showing that Next Jump was one of only three companies that they identified globally as representing the future of work; they named these future-oriented companies Deliberately Developmental Organizations (DDOs). As well, Kim's team has created a secondary social organization at the company, shepherding other companies in their process of building a better workplace culture through their Leadership Academy and bespoke tools for internal coaching, employee engagement, and shared capacity building.

 ### Kickstart Your Deep Onboarding

Look at your existing onboarding program and engage your leadership in it. Get them to talk to your new hires about your purpose, culture, and values. Have them share stories about how the culture code plays out at your organization. Talk frankly. Have them invite questions about what the culture code really means in day-to-day practice. Having the leadership there to introduce the culture shows their commitment to it and gives new employees a sense of how it plays out from the start.

Here's the Moment of Truth You've Been Waiting For

Deep onboarding is all about bringing people into the fold in a way that supports cultural growth, rather than cultural stagnation. It's about continuing to build toward alignment after you've created a framework for culture, and once you've started to hire for culture alignment. Looking at your present team, ask yourself who's on board with your cultural norms and values, and why they are there with you (or not).

I'm not suggesting that you fire or alienate people who aren't in alignment, but it's all of our jobs to notice where and when that alignment isn't taking place, so that we can discover what's possible to move forward.

Imagine the power your organization will have when you have alignment. This can only happen if your culture is genuine and if it can be communicated clearly inside and outside your doors, but also if you can support the impact of truly living the culture in your organization, with your customers, and as you build your community.

Here's an example. An amazing company, ?What If!, places a lot of focus on what they call capability and culture, but recruiting is only the first step in their process of deep onboarding. In the interview stage, they ask their candidates to do what they call "on your feet" sessions. For fifteen minutes, potential hires have to teach ?What If!'s interviewers something that they are personally passionate about. In the moments after the presentation takes place, the interviewers, which consist of a cross-sectional group, provide feedback to the candidate.

This presentation is a culture cue, not an opportunity for criticism, and employees learn just how important it is once they actually get hired. At their office, ?What If! expects their employees to provide feedback after everything. And it's not unidirectional. The culture requires that people put everything into what they do and are prepared to listen and learn from others, and also that they think critically about how they might defend their own decisions, calmly and with purpose.

CULTURE FACTS

Feedback and recognition, in a Good Culture, should always tie back to a company's core values and mission. The American Psychological Association says 89 percent of workers want to be reminded that their work has purpose and meaning. It's a leadership issue, too, because 58 percent of people leave managers, not companies. When it comes to creating a Good Culture, leaders have to show the way.

American Psychological Association, 2018

Essentially, what this company does through its onboarding process is shorten feedback loops so that work doesn't suck. The higher priority that feedback is given in a company, the earlier that problems are addressed and the more support the company creates for its employees. Keeping it constant allows for everything—praise for good work, and constructive criticism for work that can use improvement. The point is not to wait to say, "Great job," or "Let's go over your last assignment and see how you can start improving today" so that the next opportunity isn't missed. This approach, ?What If! suggests, lets employees know that any feedback sessions are for them—for anything they feel concerned about or want to work on and improve, as well as for the company as a whole. Making the feedback process positive ensures that there's a forward momentum to even the most difficult of discussions.

What this example (along with many of the other Good Culture examples in this book) shows is that the more that you can articulate your culture every step of the way during hiring, onboarding, and beyond, the more impactful your purpose will be. But it has to start from the very beginning, and your culture code has to become easy to use and follow every day after that. Connections have to be clear, and employees have to be empowered to make it work on a day-to-day basis. Your culture should drive the goals of each individual team member, and it should make sense to them. People should automatically see why they are doing what they do, rather than simply following rules.

Culture has to be designed, not imposed.

Design thinking is necessary for workplace innovation, not only because it allows us to think outside the box, but because it gets people involved and committed to culture in a way that matters to them. Remember Charlie Kim at Next Jump? Think about how his decisions changed the whole recruiting pipeline process. In a typical hiring process at his company, a department might not get their hands on new hires until six months after they start. But once those new hires are in the door, they are fully ready to thrive in that particular culture. This process, combining slow hiring and no firing, creates psychological safety for the team and the individual. It also creates a feedback culture in which people come prepared to connect with each other, be vulnerable, look at their own opportunities to contribute, and find ways forward as a team.

And it pays to be transparent.

LinkedIn has an immediate focus on culture during their onboarding process. As they explain, new hires are curious but also nervous, and their goal is to make onboarding as easeful as possible. New hires are encouraged to share not only professional but also personal facts about themselves when they are invited into the fold. They also receive LinkedIn's culture code, which is available online and details the organization's corporate, medical, and financial benefits. In addition, they are encouraged to follow #LinkedInLife across all social media platforms so that they can connect with internal brand and values ambassadors and develop the personal relationships they need to feel comfortable. As

LinkedIn states, their own research shows that it takes anywhere from six to twelve months for someone to feel fully onboarded into a company, and everyone is encouraged to be patient. Not only are new team members given backpacks and laptops set up with everything they need to get started, they are provided with a week-by-week guide for their first ninety days at LinkedIn.

Nudge Your Deep Onboarding

Buddy up incoming employees with those individuals you know are "culture carriers" in the organization from day one. Have them be the ones to show the ropes to new employees. Empower them to discuss any unspoken norms and explain how things get done at your organization. Have them tell stories about the values in action, where they've seen them rewarded, and how people are held accountable. Map both visible and invisible guidelines so that ramping up is faster and easier for everyone.

Real-Life Good Culture: Method

"Bring your weird," they said. "People are weird here."

This rallying cry, set out by sustainable consumer product organization Method more than fifteen years ago, was, well, different for a corporate values statement.

But it worked.

Sourced from their own employees, Method asked their employees to provide input into this unique values statement—one of several. And they wanted to make sure that there was clarity in how they communicated their culture, both internally and externally. They wanted to rival some of the biggest products companies in the world, like Procter & Gamble and Nestlé, but they had to do it on a tiny budget, and with the barrier of perceived inefficacy compared to more chemical-laden brands.

And that's why weird was important to them and still is. To play in a space where your main competition has some of the deepest pockets out there, you've got to play smarter rather than harder. What did that mean for Method? Self-awareness, for a start. People had to be able to come in the door knowing what made them special and uniquely qualified to be kickass-level creative, and they had to keep on building forward once they had received their onboarding training. Without that self-awareness, their team members would likely not have the confidence and innovative mindset necessary to shift the behemoths in their midst.

And to stand out, weird works.

They now have a "humanifesto"—Method's stated values, which I would categorize as a culture code. Method placed an emphasis on engaging people in creating cooperative problem-solving techniques that worked for the business and the community. In placing importance on self-awareness and well-being rather than just achievement, they created a positive work climate for the kind of work that they wanted their team to do—break the mold of what a products company ought to be doing. This was their own way of increasing the level of creativity of their team, their internal and external helping behaviors, and their job satisfaction, right from the start.

Method's culture was about truly engaging people's love of the "fight against dirty" and then attracting people who were truly suited to take up this intense journey—of which "bring your weird" was part. They didn't stop at hiring just anyone and providing employees with a set of instructions to do the work they required. Instead, the point of their approach to organizational leadership was to create the impetus for individuals to find their own pathways to achieving goals every step of the way, both for themselves and for the organization, so they could feel connected to their work and, in turn, to their company when they sat down at work.

And that means work there felt good. It didn't suck.

🌱 Embed Your Deep Onboarding

Acknowledge that culture alignment doesn't end when an employment contract is signed. Use design thinking to establish or redesign an onboarding program that not only enables employees to learn the technical skills needed to do their job, but also to deeply understand your company's purpose, mission, vision, and culture code. This needs to be not only in the content but in the way the onboarding is conducted. Your new employees need to learn not only the "what" of their new job, but also the "how work gets done."

7

Culture-Proofing

Nudging at the Pro Level

WHEN IT COMES to culture, we need to go slow. As we've all learned in our new, social-media-obsessed world, in the absence of information, people will connect the dots in the most paranoid way possible. What this means is that if you are trying to nudge a culture, there is no possibility of overcommunicating. When it comes to true and open employee development, more is more.

All of these changes take time, though.

Unlike a strategy, a culture is an ingrained set of values and ideals that ought to be common to all members of the team, and patience with culture change is likely the most important part of the process.

Here's why. Field research in business shows that it is not enough to be able to build connections between the organization's strategic business focus and new cultural requirements for their teams. In fact, simply outlining new cultural requirements is often never enough; employees will not simply take on new ideologies and points of view without the proper support systems in place. A culture that has not empowered its employees in the past, for example, will not have a culture that promotes and develops innovation leaders in the organization automatically by just stating it will do so going forward. Senior leader support, commitment, involvement, and alignment with other organization processes, practices, and programs, as well as accountability systems to support leader development, are all required. Shortcuts that limit the ability of the organization to adapt to the needs of employees so that they can be successful, or that limit employees in their own approaches to changing direction, will only serve to decrease the possibility of long-term success.[7]

In cultural change situations, the biggest risk is that a company will react too quickly to a culture code challenge and change their strategies before the shift has been demonstrated among their team members.[8]

There are three ways for you to avoid these pitfalls and to keep on nudging at the pro level.

First, create paths to make it easy for people to lean into, especially as the culture shifts in a new direction. The culture has to allow for the time needed to have employees open up to new ways of thinking about what they do on a day-to-day basis, but it also needs to ensure that employees who have good ideas remain safe within the organization. This means that employees need to receive active support for their ideas, even when these ideas are not what management expects, so that the process becomes iterative. It is only in this way that an organization will be able to challenge employees to do their best work while, at the same time, remaining supportive of their pathways to innovation.

Second, deliver and redeliver your purpose for the changes you've developed as a team, and articulate that vision in stories—past examples and future examples—of what you are looking to achieve. Employees cannot be handed a mandate to innovate in cultural terms without some examples of what's working. Supporting cultural change patiently also means that employees need to be given the chance to be collaborative rather than competitive within this new purpose. Instead of saying, "Yes, but ..." to a project, collaborative forms of critical thinking can also involve saying, "Yes, and ..." An employee's role ought to, in this way, be aligned with those of others so that there is ample reason to create trusting and long-term relationships within the team. In giving employees the chance to be collaborative rather than competitive, innovation can be more dynamic.

Third, leverage your kickoff and role model behavior as a leader. It ought to be a leader's role not only to recognize the best projects that capitalize on cultural change, but also the ways in which they can be combined, enhanced, or shifted in perspective through group dynamics grounded in capacity-building efforts. Any skills employees have in developing innovative changes in the organization's products and services, for example, need to be enhanced by an overall cultural shift that brings about expected outcomes, and that has to be mirrored in every step a leader takes.

And let's talk about trust for a moment.
Ask yourself these questions:

- Do you believe that there are multiple solutions to every problem?

- Do you regularly ask other people what they would do in order to achieve a goal?

- How much do you trust the other people in your life?

- Are you a cheerleader for other people's ideas?

- How committed are you to pursuing the best solution to a problem rather than your own solution?

Good Cultures are able to nudge at the pro level because their leaders and managers listen and respond with empathy, understand employees' needs and concerns, and keep clear of assuming that they know what matters to each person. This is the process by which a group develops a clear idea of the tasks, social behaviors, structures, and power dynamics of working with one another, and then collates these into a set of shared rules for the purpose of achieving goals together. This requires the members of the group to be able to trust one another, perhaps for the first time, and be willing to put effort into shared ideas and values so that they can collaborate on new decisions.

Building this type and level of trust will allow individual employees to work through individual issues and come to understand and focus on the importance of each other's contributions and the meaning of their work as a whole. This will achieve the purpose of building a team committed to mutual goals and interpersonal support over the short and the long term.

But trust can't easily happen over the phone. We have to double down on face-to-face contact. Videoconferencing technologies have become so easy, and they are a good second method if face-to-face is impossible or too costly in this world, but we can make them more effective in aligning culture if we put some effort into it. For example, norms to include people who are "conferencing in" can include elements like having an "on-the-line first" rule—the person who is on the phone gets to comment first. Or by assigning "in-person" buddies in the conference room who are watching out for the participation of those phoning in. These are just small examples of ways to promote inclusion and trust when video is the best option available in the moment.

In order for true cohesion to happen, and for people to feel like they are part of the solution, it is also important for a team to manage its own communication mechanisms. What kind of actions promote effective communication within a team? While technologies like email and direct messaging allow teams to communicate quickly, face-to-face meetings allow individuals to react to more than simply words: facial expressions and body language are important indicators of how people are feeling about decisions. Since everyone is different and has their own individual communication patterns, meeting face-to-face can allow people a deeper understanding of their colleagues' motivations and ideas, and even allow them to react more quickly to opportunities for discussion. This strategy will build team cohesion by ensuring that individuals build a sense of togetherness and mutual understanding.

This is especially important when it comes to managing diversity in an organization. Subconscious assessments of employees with diverse backgrounds may result in outcomes that could lead to deleterious job-related challenges for minority or out-group members, such as a lack of mentors, stalled careers, and lower performance evaluations, among other challenges. This can ultimately lead to additional stalls in organization goals if valuable individuals leave organizations in which their opportunities are limited. It can also result in the isolation of individuals or groups of people within the organization, with the ultimate result being a lack of motivation.

That really sucks. Both for people and for the organization. It's not fair, and it's a symbol of erosion of what ought to be fundamental values for any company.

Trust has to come first. When we are supporting each other, trust leads to cohesion, and that's just another way we know that our culture-proofing process is working.

 ## Kickstart Your Culture-Proofing

Look at your set of defined values and develop the behaviors you are looking for that would exemplify those values through your performance management strategy. In addition to traditional performance goals, begin to include goals and tracking mechanisms around the desired behaviors. For example, if you've identified collaboration as a value, you might list the behaviors you would like to witness that support that. For example, does an employee spend time in seeking out diverse opinions? Do they ask for others' input on their own solutions? Add a goal or objective into your evaluations that matches each of your stated values.

Cohesion can only be achieved if group members believe that they are all taking part in the same challenge together. It's about taking the time to recognize that people at many different levels of the organization are instrumental in achieving organizational objectives, not simply those in assigned leadership positions. A cohesive approach to gainsharing and compensation, for example, would not simply focus on the contributions of those in executive roles, but rather on how the members of each internal team could be recognized for their contributions. This means that teams must open discussion to all members, bring in checks and balances to ensure everyone has a voice in the process, and create a process where all members are given recognition for their roles and their personal and professional accomplishments. That way, whether the team is successful or finds that they need to revisit their methods, praise or blame cannot be attributed to a single member, as this would destroy cohesion.

The purpose of this culture-proofing process is to instill a sense of responsibility and ownership in the organization in which all team members can contribute and can be seen as contributing their diverse skills to business outcomes.

Real-Life Good Culture: Delancey Street Foundation

Delancey Street Foundation, based on their own mandate, serves the bottom 2 percent of the population in their San Francisco treatment and residential center. They're a nonprofit organization that provides rehabilitation services and vocational training for substance abusers and convicted criminals, and they don't run on grants from the city or from anyone else. Sure, they'll accept personal donations, but Delancey Street, as it's locally known, is making most of its money off its own businesses. They sell Christmas trees, and they have restaurants, a catering company, a moving company, an events facility, and the list grows every year. All of these businesses are profitable and thriving.

Here's the twist.

All of these businesses are run by Delancey Street's residents. In fact, everyone who works in Delancey Street, from program management to business leadership, is a resident except for their founder, Mimi Silbert. Their motto is: "Each one teach one." Even if a resident has only been there for thirty minutes, they're expected to have already learned something that they can teach to someone else.

Delancey Street brings people in, off the streets and out of prison, to break all of their mental models of what's possible in life.

And that's why, in order to get into the program, potential residents have to apply, and they are interviewed by other residents. Only four out of every eleven applicants get into the program. The people that other residents think can make it and can benefit from the program get to walk in the door. Although there are some immediate dropouts, for those who stay for the minimum two years, there's a 99 percent success rate.

Delancey Street changes the world, one person at a time, through community, collaboration, and cooperation.

Nudge Your Culture-Proofing

Put reminders of your values and culture code in visible places, and in meetings or in one-on-ones, highlight simple stories of values in action where possible. This could happen in any discussion as to what went right, or wrong, with a new project or an old product. Leaders should take advantage of any opportunities they have to note alignment or misalignment with the culture, in every development or performance conversation, starting from the launch of your culture code. This will cue and confirm with all other team members that the leadership team is serious about holding people accountable and rewarding people for culture-related behaviors.

Real-Life Good Culture: Zappos

The online retailer Zappos has seen a significant amount of success for over a decade. As noted by their own CEO, the company has taken a completely different approach to customer service, which has been linked to building on organizational learning rather than having a controlled strategy.

As CEO Tony Hsieh has said, "At Zappos we don't hold reps accountable for call times. (Our longest phone call, from a customer who wanted the rep's help while she looked at what seemed like thousands of pairs of shoes, lasted almost six hours.) And we don't upsell—a practice that usually just annoys customers. We care only whether the rep goes above and beyond for every customer. We don't have scripts, because we want our reps to let their true personalities shine during every phone call, so that they can develop a personal emotional connection with each customer."[9]

Unlike most call centers, which focus on canned dialogue and the shortest possible call durations, Zappos makes it a priority to allow each call center representative to do what they need to do to help make a difference in customers' lives. This flexibility allows the organization to learn from their experiences and devise better ways of customer service over the long term. It is this approach that has allowed the company to become adaptable and therefore retain its customers. The company even demonstrated growth over the course of the global economic crisis. As one pundit explained it, "It's hard to describe the level of energy in the Zappos culture—which means, by definition, it's not for everybody. Zappos wants to learn if there's a bad fit between what makes the organization tick and what makes individual employees tick—and it's willing to pay to learn sooner rather than later."[10] In other words, there is an underlying commitment, not only from the employees but from the leadership team at the organization, that allows each of the individuals involved to be focused on positive forward momentum.

There is a difference between Zappos and other organizations in the industry because their employees are excited about customer service due to the fact that they have some flexibility to work with customers to cocreate the best way to do business. In other words, high-performance cultures are those in which team members are able to thrive on constant change, rather than be challenged by it. This is only possible when autonomy is at the heart of the worker culture; controlling employees under a strict strategic regime is only going to backfire over the long term, but letting employees take the wheel on the culture drives a whole different set of results.

Your Inspiration Journey

One of our favorite things to do at FLYN is to reveal the inner workings of Good Cultures through what we call Inspiration Journeys. Four times a year, we invite all of our clients to sign up for a tour in San Francisco or New York to look at organizations we believe have innovative work practices, around a cultural theme. We generally visit four to five "host organizations" who graciously let us get a behind-the-scenes look at what they do when it comes to workplace innovation. We've visited the biggies—Slack, Airbnb, Google, Facebook, LinkedIn, Workday, Pinterest —and some you may not have heard of that are really pushing the envelope when it comes to creating Good Cultures. We dig into important questions: what works and what doesn't? What can we learn from each other? What kind of values resets really work?

After each visit we have every participant write down what they have learned, looking beyond attracting and retaining talent to tying talent to the overall goals of the organization, driving innovation through diversity in the talent pool, and developing people for the future of work. At the end of the visits we then facilitate a theming process to get deeper insights across the visits, and we help our clients translate those into potential actions back at their own organizations. It's fantastic to see what emerges and what we'd never thought of before we, as a community, critically assessed what was outstanding in our culture building.

On one of these journeys, we had a participant from Airbnb, a native Kiwi, who told us that she had never dressed up for Halloween as a child in New Zealand. Newly transplanted to the San Francisco HQ, she wasn't sure of the protocol at Airbnb, so she asked her colleagues to spill. After many assurances that everyone would dress

CULTURE FACTS

According to Gallup, in 2019, 85 percent of employees are not engaged or are actively disengaged at work. The economic consequences of this global "norm" are approximately $7 trillion in lost productivity: 18 percent are actively disengaged in their work and workplace, while 67 percent are not engaged. That's a big problem. Those disengaged employees are just putting in the time to get through the day and collect their paycheck. Turning engagement around comes from great leaders and managers who display genuine care and concern for their people and who build strong, trusting relationships where employees feel heard and supported. As leaders, the next step for growth has to come from stepping outside of your own environment to learn from other organizations.

Gallup's State of the Global Workplace report, 2019

up, she still wasn't sure. She tucked a costume into her bag that day and walked into their big, open-space office.

And there was a banana talking to a taco.

It was, in fact, a serious meeting she was watching. The heated conversation meant that arms were flailing, and PowerPoint was clicking, but there was no denying that these folks were committed to their Halloween looks—and to their company. Airbnb allows for individualism, which is embedded into their purpose and business. Different opinions are welcome, and these team members were, in fact, doing their jobs well.

Jill Macri is the former Head of Global Recruiting at Airbnb. I asked her how they embedded values into the attraction and recruitment process so that they had a culture-aligned team from the get-go.

"We designed what we called our candidate journey, which is now common recruiting lingo, around our values," Macri explains. "The value of 'be a host' was the core value to recruiting. Our mission statement was that we were going to be the ultimate host. So, for Airbnb, interviewing is not about grilling the person; it's a two-way process. Host values are very empathetic values."

And what does that really mean?

"Let's put ourselves in the candidate's shoes for a minute," Macri explains. "In coming in for an interview, they are probably lying to their boss about where they are, or they're taking a precious sick day. We think our time is valuable, but their time, in coming in to see us, is actually more valuable than ours. They're taking a risk. Our recruiting coordinators would always put their cell phone number on the whiteboard and tell candidates that at any point during their day of interviews, they could always just text. It's important that candidates don't feel unsure or insecure in any way."

Macri now has her own recruiting strategy company, Growth by Design Talent, where she and her partners work with clients to help them create recruiting practices and strategies that support the business and culture the organization is building. One of the most interesting values exercises that Macri leads for culture-proof nudging is a way to solidify the meaning, rather than the words, around a company's core values.

Macri asked team members to take one of the company's values and find an online photograph of what that value looked like to them.

"And then we compared them all. And it was hilarious. Totally different across the board. What we learned was that, in terms of defining the values, you can't assess for everything. We can only assess for your differentiators, things that are assessable in an interview process."

What matters in this example is how this little exercise was a simple, doable means to nudge their culture-proofing. People are different, but in looking at the meaning behind the values for everyone, Macri was able to bring people together and critically examine what those values looked like; how they were lived by the people in the company; what mattered about the values; and how the team imagined the values could be applied in the future, now that they had shared their perspectives together. It was simultaneously a team-building exercise and one that allowed for a deeper look at cultural norms in the company.

Real-Life Good Culture: Workday

By 2019 Workday, a leader in enterprise cloud applications for finance and human resources, was able to announce that it had reached the number four spot on *Fortune*'s list of the 100 Best Companies to Work For, up three spots from the year before. The company, founded in 2005 by David Duffield and Aneel Bhusri, lists the value of employees as number one on its ranking of core values.

And they live these values. Workday's values aren't a pathway to marketing, and they're not just a list of "nice things we want" that get new recruits in the door. Their managers are "people leaders," so named in order to remind everyone, every day, of what matters. Their teams are cross-functional and cross-generational, so they are prepared to drive diversity of opinion. They even offer every team member what they call "performance-enablement tools," a kit of resources that anyone can draw on when they need help, and to ensure that everyone can build their own professional-development platform based on their specific interests on the job.

The cornerstone of Workday's culture values is their people-leadership summit. Workday people leaders come from around the world, and they split up into working groups that include employees of different genders, roles, generations, and other personal traits. This is intentional: the company knows how much a range of backgrounds can spark meaningful conversation. For two days, these groups discuss leadership and culture, build new connections, and solidify communities of practice across the company.

After the summit, Workday keeps on building forward. #FeedbackFriday allows every one of their ninety-six hundred employees to share key information about their relationship with their manager, and to reflect on their own mental and physical health and how it's affecting their work. Their weekly Best Workday Survey gives us detailed insights into the experiences and feelings of all the generations at Workday. Workday's Senior Vice President and "people and performance evangelist" Greg Pryor cites "a culture of continuous feedback" and "a responsiveness to different generational expectations" as primary drivers of Workday's popularity among its staff. "Happy employees mean happy customers," Pryor says. "That's why it's so important to have a pulse of what's going on."

Ask yourself these questions:

- Do you believe that you care effectively for your own and your employees' mental and physical health and how it's affecting work?

- Are you committed to your own value system?

- Do you ask for feedback regularly in order to renew your ideas about what is possible at work?

- Do you believe that your daily habits reflect your deepest values in life?

🌱 Embed Your Culture-Proofing

Evaluate your current process (or lack thereof) for measuring the organization's alignment with your stated purpose, mission, vision, and values, as well as your performance management (or enablement!) process. Are these tools and processes actually giving you the data you need to assess that alignment—and to understand if your employees are working toward the same objectives and goals for the organization in the way you want them to? Are you saying you want to put the customer first, but in actuality you are measuring your customer service performance on time spent per call (namely, the less time the better)?

8

And We're There

I N TODAY'S WORLD, the pace of change is quickening. Advances in technology are accelerating, and start-ups and market leaders are disrupting business models, sectors, and industries at breakneck speed. Innovation is now the norm, in every area of business, with the exception of how we work. Most organizations are moving forward with urgency around technology, without considering the effect on their people, culture, or structure—but that has to change.

You know what you need to do.

The good news is there are people like you, reading this book, and companies out there that are breaking the workplace paradigm and putting the development of their people at the center. These are maverick companies that lead with culture, lead with people development, and lead with community and caring. As trailblazers, they are reaping the rewards of strong hires, low turnover, greater profits, higher employee engagement, and industry leadership. The business impact is real, and these methods and approaches are not just theory—they're happening.

Your competitors are starting to get the picture, and these ideas are taking hold.

Real-Life Good Culture: Trader Joe's

Trader Joe's, a specialty grocery chain based out of Pasadena, California, was developed as a means to sell hard-to-find foods to a small customer base, but it has recently developed into a national collection of stores. At its start, it represented the next stage of branded products—defined as capturing the ethical character or spirit of a bohemian-meets-yuppie culture. Like its competitor Whole Foods, Trader Joe's is the kind of organization that thrives on being able to provide a lifestyle and a sense of community to its customers, rather than having a more simplistic focus on sales growth.

What seems to set Trader Joe's apart from larger chains, even Whole Foods, and the reason that the organization has been able to grow so quickly, is that the company thrives on customer service through empowered employees. Trader Joe's has the ability to tap into an ideology of equality and fair trade that makes it impossible to provide customer service that does not hold to the same intrinsic philosophy. In other words, the ethical construct of the organization means that its customers will hold the organization's internal structure to the same standards of care. If Trader Joe's did not allow their employees to be proactive and empowered, customers would see through the façade of misalignment and would no longer remain loyal to the company.

Looking at the case studies in this book, we've seen the connection between values and a people-first orientation. Good Culture companies are those where self-efficacy and shared leadership are leveraged in order to support the development of organizational capacities. Supported and independent employees ensure that an organization performs highly, because these employees also perform at a high level. Over the long term, this approach breeds a culture that allows for learning, adaptation, and personal success, which translates directly into corporate success. This can be seen to be true even under the most stringent economic and industry conditions. What works for one organization may not work for another, but at the same time there is a common thread of openness and support in the examples of organizations in this book. Good Cultures are not only authentic, aligned, and open, they proactively increase each employee's sense of self-worth through agency, knowledge sharing, and developing a positive and innovative organizational climate that is conducive to support.

So, what did we discover about Good Cultures?

Companies that care about culture care about people. Companies need to be able to create a leadership framework in which all ideas are welcome. Companies must be open to a collaborative decision-making process that renews its values every day. Companies need to design a structure so that their existing culture can grow with them.

How do we know when we've created the culture we want? Measurements help with organizational clarity, because we know that we're getting results when the needle is moving. Remember Workday? They reach out to every employee to measure what's happening on a daily basis and survey on a monthly basis. Every week. Every month. It's technical, but it allows the company to find out what they ought to be working on in each of their locations.

How detailed does it get? Workday knows that employees in their San Francisco office have a better employee experience than those only a few counties east in Pleasanton, where they have their headquarters. Their female employees in Victoria, Canada, have a more favorable opinion of the Workday culture than other women in their offices around the world. Being aware of this means that Workday is pinpointing what's next on their agenda. Workday uses these quantitative analyses to understand the difference between "culture-add" and "culture-cost," and where they might be leaving good behaviors behind. They can track changes in employee opinions based on initiatives they've started, conferences they've attended, or product rollouts.

A dynamic approach to culture metrics will allow an organization to begin to unpack some of the issues at the core of its challenges in the past, and therefore develop a new way of thinking about their human resources, their values, and their future orientation. This can involve an absolute rating system that measures culture outcomes against expectations, a relative rating approach that measures employees' or team's feedback against others in the organization, or a more dynamic approach in which these kinds of metrics are aligned with peer- and self-assessments so that there is a more nuanced approach to culture performance management in place.

 ## Kickstart Your Culture Metrics

One of the easiest things you can do to kickstart aligning your development to your culture is to ask your top employees (who are good models of your culture) what tools they need and have used to thrive. Learning from those individuals about what they've done to thrive and what they will continue to need will cue you in the right direction. If your company values innovation, top performers may point you to structures or a lack of training that don't allow them to be as innovative as possible. By homing in on the way your top people get their work done and grow in the process, you'll kickstart your needs assessment in a way that you know will align with your culture.

Although there are many ways to measure success, a number of factors consistently show up in culture metrics that are connected to common values, and these depend on the market or local environmental context, the nature of the work, the product or service an organization produces, and customer demands. Think about the kinds of metrics that might work for your company. Some of these metrics include:

- Achieving specific, named organizational goals
- Product/service quality
- Customer satisfaction

- Capacity for innovation and creativity
- Adaptation to both organizational and technological change
- Effective information sharing and communication
- Employee attraction and retention
- Effective group and individual work
- Quality of work life
- Developing internal partnerships and alliances

Once you have an idea of what you're going to measure, there are four main pathways to actually get into the numbers game and figure out what exactly is going on. These include the goal approach, the system approach, the process approach, and the multiple-constituency approach.

- The **goal approach** is the most widely used. As its name suggests, it assesses the effectiveness of an organization in terms of its success in realizing its goals. But the reality is that an organization may have numerous goals that may conflict with one another. Goal shifts may result from an organization's interactions with its environment, from internal changes, or from external pressures, and these possibilities also have to be measured.

- The **system approach** simply looks at gaps in how internal systems function and how they are linked to cultural values. It's a little more difficult to apply in open-concept organizational forms like web design or consulting, but it can help with product-oriented companies where there are obvious systems in place that rely on communication and other cultural values.

- The **process approach** focuses on organizational functioning and integration at a departmental level. Under this approach, an organization's cultural effectiveness is viewed in terms of the smoothness of its internal processes and general operations based on culture alignment.

- Under the **multiple-constituency approach,** the opinions of the various constituent groups of an organization are considered in determining the effectiveness of the organization. This is the kind of approach that we saw at Workday in the last chapter, where people were asked how they were feeling both weekly and monthly. It's a real-time snapshot of what's going on with stakeholders, mapped to a survey method that makes comparisons easy.

Because culture is a nuanced social form, numerical metrics aren't the only way to find out if your efforts are landing where they should. When your purpose is not clearly defined, cultural outcomes can be harder to measure, and conversation is a good way to get started.

For example, measuring employee development and its links to performance may be one way of getting deep into the nuanced aspects of this work. Just like values, company metrics between team and individual performance appraisals need to be at least aligned, if not the same, and support and mentoring must be individualized so that everyone on the team knows they are valued. The company culture must shift toward shared system of values as well as shared rewards, so that everyone believes they are on the same path together toward success.

This may mean that a company has to begin to shift the ways in which teams and individuals work together. Like Workday and other Good Culture companies, employing performance metrics shouldn't only be based on sales and costs, but also on the 360-degree or multiple-constituency feedback approach mentioned above. This will not only allow individuals to feel as if they are being heard, and therefore feel more empowered to make positive changes, but it will also allow the organization to assess their internal talent needs with competency models, and to identify key people to fill critical work functions that have to do with supporting work processes and staff.

Nudge Your Culture Metrics

Offering development and training opportunities that align with your culture is an excellent way to signpost what's important at your organization. For example, if you're a bank and one of your values is to understand the customer's needs, offering financial literacy for every employee during work hours signals deep importance. If you value community, allowing your employees to take "volunteer hours" during the day (that don't go against your time off) signals that importance.

What doesn't work? Short-term fixes that are deeply lacking in alignment.

Here's an example. Perhaps much earlier than anyone might have imagined, the #MeToo campaign began in 2007, brought on by the work of feminist activist Tarana Burke. In response to the ongoing issues of the sexual assault and harassment of women, and the endemic nature of the power dynamics of rape culture, Burke, among others, believed that there could be a shift in the way that these acts of violence were seen if there was a large-scale awareness of the scope and scale of these crimes against women. The collective voice of women through social media was targeted as a means by which to explore how to shift the status quo—most importantly in the workplace, due to the ways in which wage and opportunity in the workplace are affected by multiple levels of negative results for women, such as employment, economic, social, and political inequality.

But at Ernst & Young, the response, well, kind of made work suck for women even more.

According to documents shared with the *Huffington Post*,[11] Ernst & Young introduced a training program called Power-Presence-Purpose, or PPP for short, just as the most significant of the #MeToo allegations were coming to light in Hollywood and in the offices of the largest American media corporations, in June 2018. Around thirty female executives attended that PPP training in Hoboken, New Jersey. In this seminar, women were told that they would be better off to understand that their brains, well, just didn't work the same as men's. "Women's brains absorb information like pancakes soak up syrup, so it's hard for them to focus," the attendees were told. "Men's brains are more like waffles. They're better able to focus because the information collects in each little waffle square." That's why it was also important for women at the highest echelons of this office to stop "showing skin" when they got dressed in the morning and stop "rambling" in meetings so that the men could speak.

With #MeToo, the aim was for the silence behind these issues to be broken, because too many women would have been shamed into silence—or, if they chose to make their experiences known, they may have been publicly humiliated. And yet, Ernst & Young let themselves down. As a company that has positioned itself as "women positive," employing hashtags like #WomenFastForward and making the following statement to *Huffington Post*—that it "remains—a highly recognized and award-winning leader in fostering a culture that promotes inclusion and a strong sense of belonging for all . . . [and is] unrelenting in our effort to continue to set the standard for a best-in-class culture and work environment"—the proof wasn't there at the PPP. As a company, Ernst & Young didn't align those stated values to what they were doing, and they weren't measuring the impact of the PPP on their teams at work.

Instead, the media measured their success for them.

Ultimately it doesn't matter if a lack of culture alignment is a PR nightmare or not. You don't have to fly in the
face of common sense, like Ernst & Young did, in order
to create challenges at work for the people you want to
keep on board. That's why measurement is so incredi-
bly important. Sometimes, someone misses the ball. It's
worth looking closely at what you do and how you do it so
you can ensure that you're not wasting time, money, and,
ultimately, people.

As well, organizations need to look critically at who is
facilitating growth and change so that they can develop
a succession plan that matches up with their next-stage
culture code. How can we learn from employees who
embody the ideal culture? And who isn't being asked?

Culture alignment, although difficult to measure
directly, can be inferred from organizational charac-
teristics. Good Culture organizations are trusted. They
have the reputation of delivering on their promises. Their
customers are satisfied. They attract and keep talented
employees. The productivity of employees in effective
organizations exceeds that of their competitors. They
are agile and able to adapt to change. They measure
their performance and use that information to improve
processes and products. Good Culture organizations are
those that can actualize what is important to them.

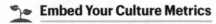 Embed Your Culture Metrics

To embed your culture code throughout your employees' journey, you need to look across the employees' experience and their life cycle, and then recognize those touchpoints in which you can develop them in a way that aligns (or doesn't) with your values. Did you prohibit someone from going to manager training because you had to get a deliverable out? What does that say about your culture and what you value? Does what is offered align with your expectations on not only the technical skills you expect your employees to have, but also the cultural norms and behaviors, the self-awareness, and the coaching they need to thrive in your organization?

9

When Does Work Not Suck?

W HEN IT COMES down to it, there are only a few things you need to remember if you want to create a Good Culture.

Work doesn't suck when we take the time to create a purpose statement that is specific about what our values are and what we believe in.

Work doesn't suck when we go on to live those values and seek out every opportunity to align our people with our values, and our values with our people.

Work doesn't suck when there is a blueprint for team members to be stakeholders in a culture development process over the long term, and when leadership isn't forcing culture in a top-down way, but rather is inclusive in putting these values into action.

Work doesn't suck when we can realize, together, that creating a new purpose and set of values is likely to be a complex matter, and one that will go through many internal iterations.

Work doesn't suck when we are clear on the way in which we value employees, customers, and other stakeholders, using empathy and psychological safety as a guide to these relationships.

Work doesn't suck when we make sure that there is a balance between our values and the utility that we want to achieve, say, through making a profit, so that there is a clear guide as to how to proceed with any challenges that take place.

Work doesn't suck when we are definitive as to how we will manage any disconnects between perceptions of value at all levels of stakeholder engagement.

Work doesn't suck when we make a commitment to measuring culture alignment, how effective our values are, and how these are applied in practice with the consent and support of our teams.

In the end, Good Cultures recognize how far we've come.

In the past, the focus of a mission, vision, and values statement for an organization was to grow at all costs, to market the organization to certain customers, to prevent risks associated with customers knowing about internal challenges, or to get the organization some good press.

While this is still true to a certain extent, the reality is that in a global market and with the advent of social media and, well, Glassdoor reviews, a company is likely to have to deal with much more than simply looking good in comparison to its peers. As well, new labor regulations are emerging, and poor business practices are being called out in public by employees as well as consumers. The companies that play to the lowest common denominator are the ones that won't last.

If we want to create a world where work doesn't suck for people, then organizations and their employees have to become part of a solution together.

In a very visible business environment, organizations have a need to examine what they are doing internally and ensure that it leads to better outcomes for their talent, and not just for their shareholders. This means putting culture to work in action-oriented plans and strategies that are measured both internally and externally. Companies can act as agents of change to drive home a collective purpose. A company needs to ensure that there is a high level of engagement from the top of the organization down, from leaders to all staff members worldwide, in order to be successful in culture coding. Not only do all employees need to become aware of the cultural expectations of the organization, but they have to believe that it matters. Values only become ingrained in the company's culture when an onboarding, development, and monitoring process takes place and values are introduced and supported by performance metrics with specific goals in mind. All processes need to be evaluated closely on a regular basis in order to see whether there is culture change taking place. A focus on culture and alignment works because businesses must develop tools to ensure they operate according to the expectations that we all want in the future, which is to make sure that we're happy and healthy, not just "calling it in."

An organization that puts culture first willingly is one that will be able to manage its own market sustainability, talent management and succession, resource allocation, and consumer interaction in a way that leads to better outcomes for everyone.

And your willingness to engage in culture alignment is, ultimately, what all of your employees want and need to succeed.

Success for employees and success for your organization is within your reach.

Acknowledgments

THIS BOOK WAS a long time coming. And it wouldn't have happened if it weren't for the following people:

My mentors, Seth Godin and Maynard Webb, who both came into my professional life at critical junctures and remain strong reminders to follow my heart's path, always.

Dimitra Manis and Annmarie Neal, thank you for giving me not only coaching, guidance, and friendship, but the model of a powerful and generous female leader.

My "team." Authoresses—you women are amazing! Special shout out to Denise Brosseau and Sarah Granger for creating this magical group.

Page Two—this book literally would not exist without you. Thank you for "pulling it out of me" as I asked you to do when we first met. Lisa Thomas Tench, my cowriter, and the whole team at Page Two—Trena White, Peter Cocking, Jennifer Lum, Caela Moffet, Meghan O'Neill, Deanna Roney, Christine Savage, Alison Strobel, Lorraine Toor, and Jessica Werb.

My local support, "OSDers" and beyond. Thank you for making me laugh and loving me through it all!

My Penn State "Raucous Retirees," Rich Bundy, Adam Dombchik, Kimberly Harris, Joe Henwood, Katie Houtman, Joe and Joannie Jorczak, Matt McKelvey, Sean Ness, Tom O'Keefe, Hutch Pegler, Jim Ryerson, and Kristin Williams. How lucky we are to have found each other in the halls of the HUB. You are forever my people, and it would take another whole book to write about how each of you have helped me grow.

My sister-coaches: Toni Cusumano Binetti, Bobbie Chapman, Mary Erskine, Julie Hassett, Michelle Tillis Lederman, Steffani Fort LeFevour, Joannie Jorczak, Maria Ross, Aimee Terosky, Laurie Burkland Waller, and all the women in Seth's FeMBA group—these are the best of the best, and I treasure every moment you've ever given to nurture and guide me.

Maria Ross, thank you for your love, support, and friendship. You are an inspiration.

Our FLYN team, Ila Asplund, Cynthia Burgess, Kimberly Harris, Jen Hothenrichs, and all our partners, collaborators, and clients. Thanks for making being "FLYNny" a powerful thing by living our values. You unlock my smile at work every day.

And finally, my partner, Decio Mendes. I'm so lucky to be able to do this work with you and the FLYN team and our clients that we love so much! You are truly THE BEST partner I could have ever asked for.

Notes

1   Ivan W.H. Fung et al., "Safety Cultural Divergences among
    Management, Supervisory and Worker Groups in Hong Kong
    Construction Industry," *International Journal of Project Management*
    23, no. 7 (October 2005): 504–12. https://doi.org/10.1016/
    j.ijproman.2005.03.009.

2   Ashley Feinberg, "Internal Messages Show Some Googlers Supported
    Fired Engineer's Manifesto," Wired, August 8, 2017, https://www.
    wired.com/story/internal-messages-james-damore-google-memo/.

3   Nancy M. Schullery, "Workplace Engagement and Generational
    Differences in Values," *Business and Professional Communication
    Quarterly* 76, no. 2 (March 2013): 252–65. https://doi.org/10.1177/
    1080569913476543.

4   Mario Buble, Ana Juras, and Ivan Matić, "The Relationship between
    Managers' Leadership Styles and Motivation," *Management:
    Journal of Contemporary Management Issues* 19, no. 1 (2014): 161–93.
    https://www.semanticscholar.org/paper/THE-RELATIONSHIP-
    BETWEEN-MANAGERS%27-LEADERSHIP-AND-Buble-Juras/0578
    2a3b4144e1f64730e976e1151daf24493ebe.

5   Zhen Cheng, "Research on Recruitment Model Based on Person-
    Organization Fit," *International Journal of Business Administration* 5,
    no. 2 (2014): 126–31. https://doi.org/10.5430/ijba.v5n2p126.

6   James Clawson, *Level Three Leadership: Getting Below the Surface*,
    4th ed. Upper Saddle River, NJ: Prentice Hall, 2008.

7   Christopher B. Dobni and Mark Klassen, "Advancing an
    Innovation Orientation in Organizations: Insights from North
    American Business Leaders," *Journal of Innovation Management* 3,
    no. 1 (March 2015): 104–21. https://doi.org/10.24840/
    2183-0606_003.001_0009.

8   Beverly A. Dugan and Patrick Gavan O'Shea, "Leadership
    Development: Growing Talent Strategically," *SHRM-SIOP Science
    of HR White Paper Series* (February 2014). https://www.shrm.org/
    hr-today/trends-and-forecasting/special-reports-and-expert-
    views/Documents/SHRM-SIOP%20Leader%20Development.pdf.

9   Tony Hsieh, "How I Did It: Zappos' CEO on Going to Extremes for
    Customers," Harvard Business Review 88 (July/August 2010):
    1–10. https://hbr.org/2010/07/how-i-did-it-zapposs-ceo-on-going-
    to-extremes-for-customers.

10 Marc Silvester, Mohi Ahmed, and Tom Brown, "The Future Belongs
    to Us All," *Business Strategy Review* 19, no. 4 (December 2008):
    12–16. https://doi.org/10.1111/j.1467-8616.2008.00557.x.

11 Emily Peck, "Women at Ernst & Young Instructed on How to Dress,
    Act Nicely around Men," *Huffington Post*, October 21, 2019, https://
    www.huffingtonpost.ca/entry/women-ernst-young-how-to-dress-
    act-around-men_n_5da721eee4b002e33e78606a.

About the Author

A WORKPLACE CRUSADER WITH more than twenty years of experience in change management leadership, Rebecca Friese transforms organizations. By identifying outdated practices from the ground floor to the boardroom, Rebecca helps everyone, from Fortune 500 behemoths to hopeful start-ups, build the capacity to implement market-leading cultural changes. Having taken on every role from employee to a consultant to Vice President of People, she knows what it takes to chart a new course for talent management.

Now, Rebecca is on a mission to help organizations not just be better places to work, but *exceptionally innovative, engaging, and forward-thinking* places to work. She's seen what happens when work sucks for people—when top-performing employees become dejected, disengaged, and ultimately leave organizations, and leaders are left scratching their heads at why this happens more often they expected, and how it affects their bottom line. What matters to employees may be very different than what managers think. In this book, Rebecca provides a step-by-step approach to creating a Good Culture, making an impact on your people strategy and ultimately the success of your organization.

www.flynconsulting.com
www.thegoodculturebook.com
#thegoodculture
#workshouldntsuck

Made in the USA
Monee, IL
30 April 2021